SOUTHERN TREASURES

By

The members of Creative
Minds Writers Group of
Ponchatoula, Louisiana

Table of Contents

Foreword

By Kathryn Martin, Group Member

It was a happy day in 2008 when established and "wanna-be" writers from a ninety-mile radius decided to form Creative Minds Writers Group and meet regularly in Southeast Louisiana's small city of Ponchatoula.

Besides being the site of the Ponchatoula Strawberry Festival which attracts some 200,000 visitors its one weekend in April each year, the city is also known for many artists participating *all* year in the arts--visual, written, drama and music.

Our group is more like family as we meet monthly to share generously from knowledge, experience and the latest in writing while encouraging efforts and celebrating successes--whether a member has over fifty books or is brand-new, working on a first one.

Our annual Berries, Bridges and Books Writers Conference brings in top-notch authors and attendees from a five-state area.

This is our second anthology and we invite you to enjoy our stories as you meet and get acquainted with our writers, seeing the diversity of writing topics and styles.

Raccoon Kittens and Pit Bull Puppies

By Deborah Young

The days were getting longer and Dorrie could not wait for daylight savings time to start...

She hated the dark coming in at 5:00 PM because it meant that her bedtime was earlier than ever. But, she could always fool her mother into letting her stay up late in the summer because she claimed it wasn't dark enough for her to fall asleep.

She'd been home schooled since first grade when she had wrapped a baby water moccasin in an old t-shirt and brought it to school in her backpack for show-and-tell. Along with the fact she had called the principal a son-of-a-bitch, taught all the first grade boys the "F" word, and scared most of the little girls with her description of butchering hogs.

Her mother told her it wasn't entirely because of those things, but they did all add up.

Dorrie had been kicked off the bus because she refused to sit in her assigned seat. When moved to the front, she'd insisted on standing behind the driver because she didn't trust his driving.

Her mother didn't drive any more than she had to and never the twenty miles into town unless it was grocery day. She decided Dorrie could be home schooled until she was better socialized into modern society or she reached the age of 18--whichever came first.

Her mother was busy baking chocolate chip cookies. They were her son's favorite and Scott was coming home from college the next day, as always, expecting cookies.

She was dropping dough on a cookie sheet when Dorrie piped up.

"Momma, why does Mrs. Fields call me a 'tomboy'?"

"I expect it is because you like to do boy things better than girl things," replied her mom.

"Why doesn't she call Scott a tomboy? He likes to do boy things," said Dorrie.

"Scott is a boy. A tomboy is a girl, like you, who enjoys doing things outdoors."

"I want you to tell Mrs. Fields I don't want to be called a tomboy anymore," said Dorrie.

"I think she would believe it more if you told her yourself," said her mother.

"I can't," said Dorrie. "I might say something that would make her mad and then you'd be angry with me."

"Well," said her mother, "You'll just have to practice on me what you are going to say to her."

"I could practice all day with you but if she argues with me I might say something I didn't practice. It all might hit the fan," said Dorrie.

"Well, maybe I'll talk to her first and then we'll see," replied her mother.

Dorrie snuck around behind her mother, quickly sticking her finger into the bowl of cookie dough and pulling out a taste.

"I don't want to learn to cook and clean or sew or have babies."

"How did babies come into all of this?" asked her mother.

"Babies are a lot like being stuck in creek mud and you are almost to solid ground but you just can't quite make it out," said Dorrie. "You never get out of the mud do you, Mom?"

" I like being in the creek mud with you," said her mother.

"You're just saying that because the hospital doesn't have a return policy after nine years," said Dorrie.

"Well, you have a long time before you have to decide on babies," said her mother.

"Why did you wait so long to have me?"

"Well," said her Mother, "your father and I wanted to wait until we had plenty of time for another baby. Scott was ten when you were born, so he was older and didn't need as much raising up."

"I think it was because you couldn't afford two kids at the same time. Scott needs so many expensive things, like tuition, cars, and money for dates. I'm thinking he's going to bankrupt the family and I'll have to go live with Aunt Tootie," announced Dorrie.

"Dorrie, you don't even have an Aunt Tootie! I don't know where you get these ideas," said her mother.

"I bet if I had an Aunt Tootie, she'd let me have a Pit Bull puppy."

"I doubt that very much," said her mother. "Most 'Aunt Tooties' I know are more opinionated than your father."

"You do know I'd be totally happy with a Pit Bull puppy and would never ask for anything else until I started high school," said Dorrie, trying to make a point.

"I am sure you would need other things. Besides, a Pit Bull puppy would take up a lot of your time in care and training."

Dorrie was tired of talking and decided she'd better go outside to the barn to look for vermin lurking around.

The machinery shed had become a haven for rats because her father was allergic to cats. After the last mouser died her father had declared no more cats. Even the barn ones were banned. Her father would rather use poison instead of letting Mother Nature and a few cats take care of the problem.

Dorrie trotted toward the shed and carefully crept inside. Within a few minutes she was making enough noise to wake the dead. She started toward the house like she had been shot from a rocket launcher.

Her mother looked up from her cookies and rushed to the door. She could hear the screams. Fortunately, with Dorrie, screams didn't necessarily mean anything serious.

"Momma, I found a nest of raccoons in the machinery shed. They're in the east corner up in the roof support. Please, go catch me up one. They don't have their eyes open yet. I can tame a little one down real fast. I know you got some leather gloves somewhere."

"No, I am not going to climb up in the rafters and get you a baby raccoon. It is just fine where it is with its mother. I thought Grandpa said you can't have a raccoon."

"No," said Dorrie. "Grandpa said no 'S' words. No skunks, no spiders, no snakes. A raccoon is fine. Please, Momma, catch me up just one. If I can't have a Pit Bull puppy, I don't know why a raccoon can't be a compromise. Daddy says compromise is everything in a business deal."

"Now, if I caught one," said her mother, "that momma coon would be so mad she would come after me and tear me up before I could get down off the ladder. You know how Grandpa's big old coon dog, Rachet, got torn up by that sow coon. He went after the tree where her babies were hidden and she almost tore his ear clear off. Doc Eddie had to sew it back on and Rachet had to stay in the animal hospital for three days. Have you forgotten?"

"No, Momma. But, you're smarter than Rachet and I can be your lookout. We can get a baby before she comes back. I can keep it in my room in a wooden box and we have plenty of towels to make it a nice pallet to sleep on."

"Really," said her Mother. "What are you going to feed it? Where can you buy raccoon milk? You can't feed it crawfish out of the ditch or grapes from the store since it doesn't have its eyes open yet."

"Doc Eddie has milk replacer for kittens. I'm sure he has something for raccoons."

"You'll just have to call Doc Eddie and see if he has milk replacer for raccoons."

"So, you aren't going to get one for me today."

"No, I don't believe I am," said her mother.

"Well, I'm going to head out to the mailbox and see if the mail has come yet. Maybe Daddy has sent me something from somewhere."

Dorrie paused and began again, "You know, if Daddy stays away much longer, I'm not going to recognize him when he walks through the door. I might mistake him for an intruder and just shoot him before he has a chance to say, 'I'm home'."

"Just what are you planning to shoot him with?" asked Mother.

"Well, I have my pellet gun. I'm getting pretty accurate with it. Grandpa put up an aluminum pie plate in the peach tree and I hit it four times out of five," said Dorrie.

"That's wonderful. I am sure Grandpa is very proud," her mother said before reminding her, "Your father's current picture is on the bookcase. Anytime you feel your memory is fading, you can just refer to the photo and commit his face to memory again."

"I'm not saying I'd shoot him for sure. But, there is always a chance I might get scared and just react in the middle of the night."

"I don't think your father is going to come home in the middle of the night. I will be sure to let you know when he is coming in and you can put the pellet gun in the gun safe so no one will get hurt."

"Well," said Dorrie, "I really need to keep my gun under my bed because you never know when a real intruder might just get in this house."

"I am sure you will protect and serve this household in an excellent fashion while your fa-ther is out of town."

Dorrie sat at the table, watching her mother fold chocolate chips into the cookie dough. Be-ginning to get bored, she jumped down off the kitchen stool saying, "I better go out and check on those chickens. They may have laid some eggs I missed last night."

Dorrie checked on the chicken coop, the one built by her Grandpa that would repel any predator. He'd even concreted the wire into a trench so nothing could dig into the coop from beneath.   Lifting the door to the nest boxes, she found four eggs. She'd forgotten the egg bas-ket so she'd have to get them later.

Things looked good, but she did find some tracks that looked like fox or maybe coyote. She liked the chickens, but mostly she liked their eggs. She really didn't want any of them to be lunch for some four-legged villain. She decided she needed only to head to the woods and look for more signs of predators.

Just as she was pointed toward the woods, she heard an awful noise that sounded like a crash.

Running toward the front of the house, she saw a huge car pulled off the road and a man sitting in the driver's seat. As she got close, she could see he was wearing hunting camo and was yelling into his cell phone.

"Get a damn wrecker out here now or I'll have your ass! Don't cut out on me! Okay, I'm not sure where I am. Hello! Hello!"

Dorrie was excited. She'd not had a captive audience for almost six months. At least not since she lined concrete blocks across the road causing the Fed Ex driver almost to crash his delivery truck. Her father wasn't home when that happened. But, he'd given her a good chewing out on the phone. He'd told her someone so irresponsible would never be able to earn a puppy. That had sobered her up enough to take concrete blocks off her list of things to do when she was bored.

New people to talk to and find out what is going on in the rest of the world was always welcome so she walked right up to the driver's side.

He didn't see her because he was rummaging in the glove compartment trying to find his Triple A card.

Dorrie tapped on the window calling, "Hi, do ya need some help?"

The driver was yelling at his phone, "Better yet, you find me a car dealership! Wait! Great, I lost him!"

Finally looking up, he saw Dorrie and said, "Hello, little girl. Do you have a phone book?"

"I don't know." said Dorrie. "What does it look like?"

"It's a phone book. It might be yellow," said the driver.

"I'll go ask my mom and be right back," said Dorrie.

She ran back to the house and found her mother taking a load of clothes out of the dryer.

"Do we have a phone book?" she asked.

"Somewhere," said her mother. "What do you need with a phone book?"

"I don't need one. But, the man in the broken-down car needs to call a wrecker."

"What man in what broken-down car?" she asked, adding with suspicion, "Have you strung barbed wire across the road again? The last time you did that, Mr. Woolverton got barbed wire wrapped around his axle and Grandpa had to come over and cut it off with bolt cutters. Did you put concrete blocks across the road?"

"I most certainly have not. This junker quit on its own," said Dorrie. "I will not put concrete blocks across the road again. Daddy tore into me while he was waiting for his plane in Miami to take him to Haiti."

"Dorrie, your father has never been in an airport in his life. He was not going to Haiti, the country. He was going to Hayti, Missouri, the city. He was selling barge equipment on the river," said her mother. "Where do you get these ideas?"

"'Haiti' sounded a lot better. 'Hayti' is a little nothing town. They don't even have a beach."

"Here, take the phone book out to him. He probably doesn't have any service out here. I'll come out and take a look after this last sheet of cookies comes out of the oven."

14

Dorrie ran back to the car with the phone book. When she got there the man had the hood up and was checking the motor. She could hear him cursing under his breath.

She handed him the phone book, asking, "What do ya think is wrong? You might check the battery terminals to see if they're loose. It could be a bad battery. You know these new batteries just quit on you without any warning."

"I know what's wrong," he said. "It's the main belt that drives everything. I'm going to need a mechanic."

"We could call my grandpa," said Dorrie. "He knows lots of mechanics."

"Why didn't you say something before? He could already be here."

"My mom is coming out as soon as the cookies are done. Where are you from, Mister?"

"I'm from Des Moines."

"What are you doing here in another state?"

"Looking at property to build a hunting lodge."

"That sounds like a big job," said Dorrie. "You going to build it all by yourself?"

"No, I have a partner who will design and build it."

"My Grandpa built a chicken coop. Wanna go see it?"

"Maybe later. Can we walk to your house so I can use the phone? We could call your grand-pa about a mechanic."

"All right," said Dorrie. "Grandpa lives just around the corner. He can be here in two shakes."

They headed toward the driveway but soon the man acted like he was getting winded so Dorrie sat down on a stump and the man sat in the wicker chair next to the new waterfall feature that Dorrie's mother had just had to have.

He took out a cigarette and pulled a lighter out of his pocket. On the lighter was a pretty young lady winking at its holder. The words, "Come & See Me" were printed across the bottom.

Dorrie caught him out of the corner of her eye and yelled. "What are you doing? Don't you know smoking gives you cancer? It's on the TV every day."

He knew this kid couldn't be over ten but she acted more like forty.

They sat there in silence.

Dorrie couldn't take it any longer, "You got a dog?"

"Yeah, a Brittany Spaniel."

"What's its name?" asked Dorrie.

"Her name is Rose. I take her when I hunt quail at a game reserve in Texas."

"That's a nice name," said Dorrie. "I don't have a dog."

"That's too bad. All kids need a dog," said the man.

"I don't imagine I'll ever have a dog until I get shed of this place and on my own," said Dorrie.

"Maybe you just need to ask," the man suggested.

"My daddy won't hear of buying me a Pit Bull puppy. I have asked every summer since I can remember and he always says no. I asked for a German Shepherd, a Doberman, and a Husky. I got the same answer. He says I can have a Shih Tzu or a Cockapoo. Now, does that sound like a dog any self-respecting person would want to own? I don't know how you can keep from being embarrassed when you tell people you have a Cockapoo."

The man looked thoughtful, then said, "Maybe, if you asked for a dog with a better reputation your dad might change his mind."

"I've had my heart set on a Pit Bull puppy since I was four years old. How can you just give up a dream?" asked Dorrie.

"Well, maybe you aren't willing to meet him halfway," said the man.

"I tried to be reasonable today and have my mother catch me up a baby raccoon. One with its eyes still closed. But she's just as bad as my daddy."

"I'm not sure a raccoon kit is much better than a Pit Bull puppy," said the man.

"You grownups are all alike. I could just spit, you make me so mad," said Dorrie.

The two walked on toward the house, getting to the driveway just as Dorrie's mom turned the corner.

The driver in the camouflage t-shirt was looking things over, wondering where in the hell that last turn had taken him. This was so far off the beaten path, he wasn't sure how to get back to the main road. These roads might have been blacktop at one time but now they were three quarters dirt and one quarter gravel. He was looking for a secluded mansion without a burglar alarm. He had it on good authority there were plenty of things to acquire for resale.

"Dorrie, get over here and bring that man with you!" shouted her mother.

The two started up the dusty driveway. While Dorrie practiced kicking rocks, the driver stopped at the mailbox looking for an address or some road number for Triple A.

"What can we do for you?" Dorrie's mother asked.

She kept her right hand in her pocket. Dorrie hoped her mom had listened to her and was keeping her finger out of the trigger guard of her old pistol.

"Well, Ma'am, if you could call someone to come out and look at my car or if you know someone who has a wrecker, I would be very grateful," said the driver.

"Let me go in and call my father. He can come over and figure out what's the best plan," said her mother. "Dorrie, you come back to the house with me."

"Mom," said Dorrie, "I was just going to show him the chicken coop. Why do I have to come with you?"

"Because we don't know anything about him, so you are with me for now."

Dorrie's mother got her father on his cell. He was on the tractor bushhogging but said he'd be right over and gave her instructions.

"You stay in the house until I get there. Got your revolver? Use it if you have to."

"Yes, Dad, I have my gun. But I think it ought to be Dorrie that has it. She's the crack shot in this family. I can't even load the clip on the new nine millimeter automatic you bought me."

"You'll be fine. Any shot in the general direction should connect with some part of him," said her father.

"Let's hope it doesn't come to that," said her mother. "He doesn't look like your average serial killer."

"Sure," said her father. "They said the same thing about Bundy. I'll be there in a minute."

It was only a ten-minute drive from the field when Grandpa pulled up in the pickup and got out.

He walked around the car looking for body damage but the car looked too new to have just given up the ghost. Looking under the hood, he could see the shredded belt but no damage to the radiator or fan when it had come apart.

The car was in great shape, clean on the inside, but under the hood was a disaster. The motor was filthy and it appeared the heads might be leaking oil. There had been no maintenance on this car.

Dorrie's grandfather spit out a stream of tobacco. He was disgusted. Anyone who took such poor care of an expensive automobile wasn't worth a plug nickel. You couldn't trust someone like that.

The man walked back to the car, introduced himself as Ronnie Blatt and started the conversation.

"I'm in the area looking for property and I got a tip there was property for sale in this area but I'm not sure I'm on the right road."

Dorrie's grandfather sized him up and could see he was trying to look like some sort of big- shot investor. The camo t-shirt was brand new. Grandpa figured if he looked in the back he might find the price tag still on it. He'd seen enough of these guys in his time to know a "bar-gain hunter" when he saw one. The man was trying to look like a good neighbor who just want-ed a place to hunt on weekends.

"Well," said Grandpa. "I took a look under the hood and your serpentine belt is shredded. I can call someone that'd know how to fix it but may not have the part."

"Whatever you can do to help me would be great." said Ronnie.

Grandpa pulled out his phone, scrolled through the contact list and hit "call".

But, there was something about Ronnie Blatt that just didn't set well. Grandpa wanted him out of the area before dark.

"Bennon Car Repairs? Can you send a wrecker over here to my daughter's house? There's a gentleman here with car trouble. He needs a tow to your garage. Okay. We'll be waiting."

"What did they say?" asked Ronnie.

"They can be here within the hour. They'll radio the wrecker driver and he can come back this way."

Dorrie had snuck out the back door and crept through the shrubs until she got to the black-berry patch. She could stay inside the row of canes and no one would ever suspect anyone was eavesdropping on the conversation.

"I'm mighty thankful for your help," said Ronnie. "I still haven't found that piece of proper-ty for sale. The real estate guy said it was on several hundred acres and had a British sounding name."

"You mean 'Ballycastle'?" asked Grandpa. "The people that own it are vacation crazy. They're not home now, but I know for a fact it's not on the market."

"Really," said Ronnie. "I'd still love to look at it. Do you know what road it's on?"

"It's about a mile further down this road, then you make a left on Irish Lane and follow the road to a long driveway at the end."

"I really appreciate the information," said Ronnie.

Grandpa and Ronnie waited for the wrecker, making small talk about the weather and the Cardinals' chances to get back in the World Series playoffs.

The wrecker arrived and the car was soon loaded up with ole Ronnie on his way to town—and they still had daylight.

Grandpa turned and headed up the drive to the house and Dorrie left the safety of the black-berry thicket to get to the back door and inside so she could find another hiding place.

"Well," Dorrie's mother asked. "Did you see him off?"

"Yes, but he wanted to know how he could find Ballycastle. I don't know what he wants, but I think he's up to no good."

"Why would you say that? He told Dorrie he was looking at property," said his daughter.

"I think he is, but not to buy," said Grandpa. "He's casing the place to rob it."

"The old Ballycastle place. Wasn't it condemned years ago after the fire?"

"Sure was," said Grandpa. "It's two counties over anyway. I sort of mentioned it was down this road and then take a left on Irish Lane and it's the last driveway on the right."

"Dad, you did not! Our county sheriff lives at the end of Irish Lane!"

"I didn't want him to have to go looking for robbers," said Grandpa. "I thought this time I'd just send them his way."

"You're worse than Dorrie," said his daughter. "You have to fix this."

"I'm going to call the sheriff and let him know I set up the sting."

Dorrie was hiding in the hall closet and knew this was more exciting than stringing barbed wire across the road or finding a nest of raccoon kittens.

This would be a perfect time to practice her detective work!

She had lots of things to do before dark...

She had to get her pellet gun and pellets, dress all in black like they did on TV, and she needed to practice a commanding voice. She didn't have much time.

Grandpa was still in the kitchen talking to his daughter when he noticed a familiar aroma coming from a large Tupperware container.

"Am I smelling chocolate chip cookies?"

"You might be, since I made a double batch today for Scott," said his daughter.

"My old grandson, Scott, has it too easy. He needs to learn to share," said Grandpa. "Besides, I haven't had any lunch, so a cookie sounds pretty good."

"Would you like a cup of coffee with that cookie?"

"That would hit the spot."

His daughter handed him a steaming mug and set a plate of cookies in front of him. She watched as he smiled, picked up the biggest cookie, and bit off a chunk.

Soon after her grandpa left, Dorrie looked around in her closet to find black pants and a black turtleneck. Putting a handful of pellets in her pocket, she figured she could go to bed and not argue with her mother.

She would change clothes and get in bed and wait until dark to go out her window and head to Irish Lane. She knew the way there and back by heart and could easily make it in the dark.

* * * * *

It was Ronnie's lucky day.

The garage had the serpentine belt and within an hour, he was back out on the road. He'd found a county road map at the gas station and retraced his route to get back to Irish Lane, managing to get enough bars on his phone to call his friend. They were to meet at the local baseball park to get their plan together.

20

It was dark when the two men finally pulled up alongside each other at the park. A strong wind was blowing and the evening temperatures were going to be colder than they'd anticipated.

"Okay, here's what we're going to do," Ronnie said, laying out the map and pointing to a red line connecting the roads so they could follow the route.

"We're going to go in the house and take what we can right away. The old idiot farmer told me the owners were in and out and they aren't there right now. Look for little things you can carry out easy. Look for jewelry boxes, money, art."

"You think we can do this tonight?" asked the partner. "We don't really have time to set this up that well."

"We might not get a chance to do it again. Drive up the road and when you get to Irish Lane turn off your lights before you head up the driveway," said Ronnie. "When we get ready to leave, we're going to go our separate ways and meet up tomorrow back home at our usual place."

Professional robbers would never take separate cars to a house robbery. Even a third grader would know that was a risky move. But, intelligence and common sense hadn't stuck on either of them.

The two men drove out and when they got to Irish Lane, they turned off their headlights and drove up the long driveway to the house. About 200 feet from the garage, they stopped and turned off their engines. The house was dark and the wind had died down. They decided to go to the back of the house.

Walking near the brick patio, they felt safe, not hearing any dogs.

At the back door, they quietly cut out the pane of glass with a circular glass cutter and turned the deadbolt lock by reaching inside.

Dorrie was hidden by the moonless night as she watched the men from their arrival to their entry of the house. She was quiet as a fox casing out a hen house.

Opening the car doors, she took out the keys to both their cars. They were not going to get away! Dorrie knew she could outrun them in the dark, but she didn't think about outrunning a bullet.

The two men were in the house for less than a minute when the alarm went off. They started back the way they'd come in when the silhouette of a man holding a baseball bat appeared in the front hallway.

21

As they were backing out, Ronnie pulled out his gun and yelled at the shadow, "Stop where you are and lay down that bat!"

The figure continued to walk toward Ronnie, who fired one round at the sheriff and took aim to fire again.

They say you never hear the bullet that kills you and Ronnie didn't hear anything coming, but what felt like a bullet hit his forearm. The sudden pain caused him to drop his gun and grab his right arm.

"I'm shot!" he hollered. "I'm shot! Help me!"

The sheriff leaped forward and grabbed up the pistol, aiming it at Ronnie's accomplice whose arms came up in surrender. He got on his knees, begging the sheriff not to shoot.

After both men were handcuffed, the officer yelled at the lone figure in the doorway, "Hey, Deputy, is that you?"

"No, it's your guardian angel," yelled back Dorrie.

The two men hadn't looked behind them and didn't know Dorrie had been standing there in their only way out.

Yes, standing there smiling smugly as she calmly held her recently-fired pellet gun!

Dorrie and the sheriff were laughing when Dorrie's mother and Grandfather came in the back door finding the robbers laid out on the floor with their hands cuffed behind their backs.

"Dorcas Jane! What kind of mess have you gotten yourself into now?" demanded her mother.

"Now, she's just fine," said the sheriff. "I'm going to deputize her next time I need a crack shot."

Grandpa hooted with laughter and her mother just threw up her hands.

"Don't you ever run off to a pistol fight again!" ordered her mother. "Wait until your father hears this one!"

"I don't know why you're so mad at me," Dorrie exclaimed, waving her arms. "This is Daddy's fault anyway. This could all have been avoided.

"If I'da had me a good Pit Bull, I could'a sic'd him on the bad guys and never had to fire a single shot!"

The End

Poetry and Prose

By Tanya R. Whitney

Overlooked

Browning fronds jut out the broken vase,
Slowly dying in the dismal landscape.
Neglected and forlorn, they appear sad
To be ignored each day after day.

They quietly sway in the silent breeze
Created as the cars go speeding by.
Oblivious to life ebbing away with
The passage of time and loss of care.

Once tenderly nursed by a loving heart,
To flourish under the protective eyes
Of the one who cultivated it from
A tiny seedling to a graceful bloom.

The hands that once tended it with passion,
Have gone, leaving it without the vital
Nurturing that is needed daily to
Live and continue showing its beauty.
Deemed irrelevant and abandoned,
Left behind to fend on its own.

Like a life left alone and overlooked,
It slowly began to wither and die.

Browning leaves reach up to the sky,
Seeking sustenance and heavenly support.
Petals closed like a child's praying hands,
Its faith tested by the hardships endured.

Left without support, it will wither and die.
A lack of touch or friendly words spoken,
Shrivels its desire to shine in its beauty
And mirrors the homeless beings on the street.

Delicate blooms left to weather the elements,
Alone and without any protection.
Forgotten and overlooked as the home
Once full of love, perishes from neglect.

Autumn Leaves

A kaleidoscope of colors
Brushed across the browning landscape,
Like an artist paints the season
Of autumn on his white canvas.

Reds, oranges, and browns cascade
Up and down the treed mountainside
Dotting the immense canvas with
The hues of the coming season.

An easterly crisp and cool breeze
Blows through the colors of the trees,
Like tides roll across the ocean
With waves of fluttering colors.

Pumpkins growing on spindly vines,
Scattered across the garden beds,
Hail the upcoming holidays
With special foods of the season.

The zenith of life brought upon
The cycle of the passing time
And the joyous nature in the
Celebration of the harvest.

As the leaves change from the summer
Colors and drift down from the trees,
They bring life to the ground below,
Nourishing plants and animals.

A soft blanket to provide warmth,
Covering the forest floor and
Protection from the elements
As the icy season transpires.

Dried browned corn stalks stand forlornly,
Shucked and dried in parallel rows,
Soon to be cut down to become
Fertile soil for the future crops.

Hay bales stacked high over our heads,
Ready to mark the boundaries
Of the enormous cornfield maze
Cut to give us fun and laughter.

Autumn, a season of dying,
A time of rejuvenation,
Fiery reds, oranges and browns
Fluttering to their grave below.

Lost Faith

The steps of stone leading to the entrance
are grayed and beaten by years of usage.
Countless footsteps have carved the raised stones
into shallow cups to catch the sins of men.

A simple, unadorned wooden cross
sits above its plain mahogany steeple.
It shadows those who cross the threshold
seeking its protection and divine guidance.

Heaven's music filters from the choir loft,
voices of angels mixed with instruments.
A healing balm for souls tired and drained,
cleansing and uplifting with every note.

A simple altar arranged at the front
with the holiest of all books placed there.
It bestows life to barren hearts and minds
for all to share in its words of salvation.

The modest pews filled with the downtrodden,
sinners, young and old who seek absolution.
God's words relayed by a fervent preacher
and taken to heart by his faithful disciples.

Sunlight beams through the stained-glass panes
as the flock approaches the altar of salvation.
A ray of light shines upon the one on the cross
whose sacrifice and death cleanse stained souls.

An abiding faith lost on the battleground
and stifled in the inhumane killing fields.
It is reborn and renewed by His blood,
the past sins of the repentant are forgiven.

At peace now, a new person has been born
from His salvation and God's forgiveness.
A new soul triumphs in this battered soldier
with the mercy found in this weathered church.

Storm Clouds Ahead

Grayish billowing white clouds
Rise and roll across the skies.
One following the other
Like freight cars on a railroad.

Tall, spiny, green needled trees
Swaying in the gusty winds,
Sweep across the thrashing sky
Like a willful child's tantrum.

A violent storm brews,
Coming in from Southern shores,
Moisture and wrath gathered
In its fiery clouds on high.

Sunlight grows dim and faint
As darkened clouds amass,
Their dense elements hiding
The bright star's rays from the earth.

The weather's rampant turmoil,
Ravages the land and air,
It echoes the feelings of rage
Caused by scheming actions.

Promises made under oath
Have been shattered like the vase
Thrown upon the tiled floor in
A fit of anger and heartbreak.

The clouds blacken with despair
Much like a battered, hurt heart,
Collecting strength, thundering
As they fill the sky with tears.

Emotions build into
A towering crescendo,
Ready to explode and spill
Like the storm's teeming rainfall.

Like the lightning and thunder,
No longer able to
Contain the words or feelings
Raging in a clouded heart.

As the rain begins to fall
So do the tears, one by one.
Flooding down onto the ground
To seep into the warm earth.

Becoming one with the storm,
Passing through this moment with
Thundering roars of passion
As all vent their fury.

Upon reaching the climax,
Calm begins to sap strength.
Like the child who has grown tired
From his loud tantrum and stills.

Snow white puffy clouds appear.
The green needled trees now still,
Both, serene in the storm's end.
The intense power now dead.

The furious storm has passed
But its aftermath lingers.
Leaving tears upon the earth
To be transformed and renewed.

Tanya R. Whitney

Untitled Soliloquy

Dark oblivion, floating in mental blankness.
No beginning and no end in sight.
Questions circle and nag at
The thresholds of awareness.

Foreign thoughts invade the blackness.
Erratic and random in nature
Whirling in and out of the
Blurred edges of consciousness.

Uncontained emotions spew forth
A power struggle between good and bad.
Confusion reigns like the
Hot and cold flashes of menopause.

Internal demons shouldered alone,
Too private to share with anyone.
Grief is awkward and ugly,
Cleaned up with memorials and tributes.

Scattered feelings in turmoil.
Overwhelming blame for the sins of others.
Irritation simmers on the cusp,
Ready to explode on the unsuspecting.

Emotions that have been shoved down
Into the recesses deep inside,
Push defiantly upward past the plug
That kept them tightly contained and bottled.

Rehashed nightmares of senseless tragedies.
Visions of that final sight of a terrified face
Morphed into the mask of death's grimace.
It's etched into the mind's notebook.

The pressing memories mentally hamper
Moving forward out of the darkened abyss.
The inky darkness swallows up all feeling,
Paralyzing images that will not die.

False hope turns to desolation and despair
Bound together in the infinite void.
Taking away all dreams of regaining
Redemption and absolution in this lifetime.

Forgive Me Father

The day grows longer as time grows shorter. Waiting here all morning. It should have been ended by now, but it hasn't. I didn't want anyone to get hurt, I just wanted the pain to stop. No one understands me anymore. I don't even understand myself now. Life is no longer simple or easy. Hell, I couldn't even do this right. I planned to be gone by now but the park called to me this morning before dawn as I held the bottle in my hand. Maybe to take in one last sunrise, to feel the morning breeze on my face one last time.

The sun has risen to mid-morning. I sit alone in the crowds surrounding me, though they can't see me here. The excited screams of the children playing in the park can be heard. The loving admonishments of the mothers echo across the open field. A light breeze ruffles the leaves on the trees. Birds soar past, swooping and flitting from tree to tree as they call to each other, oblivious to the families and friends gathered below them.

No one notices me sitting here beneath the massive ancient oak tree. The centuries old roots traveling above the ground hide me from their vision. The smoke of their grills waft across the sky. But I can't smell the food. My senses are numbed, unable to differentiate the aromas. A little girl toddles close by, shyly glancing my way. I lift my hand weakly to wave. She turns and scurries back to her mother. I stare at my hand. Where did all this red come from? I try to think what it could be. I can't concentrate though. Oh yeah, I remember now, somebody shot me.

"Isn't that rich," I look up to the heavens. "I was ready to end it all. Take the pills and go peacefully to sleep forever. Instead, here I sit, a victim of crime." My laugh turns into a gasp for needed air. I ponder the irony of the situation.

The sounds of the park seem to be fading yet I can still see the children running around in a carefree game of tag. I drop my hand to rest on my leg, queries about the red forgotten. Thoughts of being robbed this morning no longer matter. I lean my head back against the knotty trunk of the tree. My eyelids are getting heavy and drift down, shutting out the sights around me. Breaths come slowly, in and out. Each movement more shallow than the last.

"Hey mister, are you okay?"

The voice of a young child penetrates the fog in my brain. I try to answer but my mouth won't or can't move. My eyes slit open to see a young boy about eight or nine years old standing at the end of the tree's overhang. I watch as he turns, hoping he'll leave me alone. No child should watch as someone dies.

"Hey Dad, come here! I think there's a dead guy over here." The boy called out as though he just found a lost puppy.

I smile inwardly. No kid, I'm not dead, at least not yet. I try to open my eyes wider but the lids have become heavy. A hand presses against my shoulder.

"Sir can you hear me? Are you okay?"

My head lolls to the side, weightless. The man pulls out his phone and calmly calls for help.

"Son, go back to your Mom," the man orders the young boy.

"But Dad, I found him!" The boy responds in a pleading manner hoping to stay.

"Go. Back. To. Your. Mother. Now!"

I faintly hear the kid scramble away grumbling something about finding the dead guy first. I try to speak again but only a grunt escapes. My limbs feel as though they are bound by chains.

"Hold on, help is on the way. Stay with me."

The hand on my shoulder grips tighter as though it's trying to keep my soul from leaving my dying body.

"C'mon man, don't die on me now." The voice becomes more worried. His movements are more urgent as he tries to stem the life seeping from my body.

I can tell when he realizes it's too late. Too much time has passed. Too much blood has soaked into the ground. No, it was not the way I planned it but maybe that's better. My family won't have to live with the stigma of a suicide. Not have to live with questions that could never be answered.

I'm glad the boy is gone. It's better that he doesn't see my last breath. No one was supposed to see it. It was supposed to be as though I went to sleep in my bed and just never woke up. However, there's a strange solace to know that I won't die alone. For the first time in a long time, I can accept that someone cares about me, even a stranger. His voice has an endearing intimacy to it. I feel his arm go around my shoulders in a half hug. From far off, a prayer is being recited. A prayer that I haven't heard in years. My eyes spring open to see the man comforting me and praying for my lost soul.

"The Lord is my shepherd..."

My eyes focus on a chain around his neck. A cross hangs from it. It glistens and shines as it sways with his movements as his words seep into my tormented soul.

"No, I shall not want..."

I feel at peace. The weight of my transgressions has been lifted off my shoulders.

"Comfort and strengthen your servant and save him through your goodness..."

A soothing warmth floods throughout my body. A blanket of grace and hope envelops me.

"I walk through the valley of death..."

As the last breath leaves my body, my last conscious thought whispers in the breeze.

"Forgive me Father for I have sinned."

Prose

By Lynette Vinet

The Answer

After clanging the cowbell summoning her husband Frank to supper, Ellie Wakeland set the table.

When Frank entered the kitchen and sat down, she carefully watched him.

His lined and weary face reflected long hours in the Louisiana heat, and his black hair was subtly turning gray.

As he playfully ruffled their son's hair, Ellie pitied him, because soon she was going to hurt him.

She watched Frank and Tommy together, aware of their special bond. Each adored the other, and as many times as Ellie had lain in Frank's arms, he thanked her for giving him such a wonderful son.

But feeling uneasy, she always turned away and faced the wall.

"I think soybeans will fetch a good price this year, Ellie," his deep voice boomed in the small kitchen after he wolfed down his meal. "If so, maybe you can buy that fancy coat you liked so much at Parker's Mercantile. Winter will be upon us before you know it, and that old brown rag you've been wearin' won't keep you warm much longer."

He smiled tiredly at her over his plate of cornbread and honey. "I want my girl to look her best."

Ellie started to clear away the dishes, pretending she didn't hear him.

"Mama, I'm goin' to Jim-Roy's. He's got a new calf I aim to see," said Tommy, who at thirteen had begun feeling independent.

"Alright, but be careful and be back before it gets too dark!" Ellie shouted at the boy's retreating back as he rushed out the kitchen door.

"He's always in such a hurry," she groused to Frank, yet she was pleased to have her son out of the way.

After a few minutes, she turned to Frank who was cleaning his teeth with a toothpick. "We got a letter today."

"Oh, who from?"

Turning her back, she scraped the remnants of Tommy's food into the garbage can.

"From your brother."

He stopped picking his teeth, and it seemed forever before he spoke.

"What'd the bastard have to say?"

She winced under his steady stare.

"Only that he's coming for a visit to see you and Tommy...and me. It's been a long time."

"Yeah, about fourteen years," he remarked while Ellie wiped an imaginary stain from her jeans. "Can't imagine why Pete's taken a notion to visit after all this time."

Frank stood and threw the toothpick in the trash then kissed Ellie on the back of the neck. "Goin' to take a bath and hit the sack. Got to get up early in the mornin'."

Frank left the room, and soon Ellie heard the rush of water through the pipes as Frank prepared his bath.

"Dumb ox," she whispered under her breath. "Pete's coming for *me*."

She carelessly tossed a dish in the sink, causing it to crack in the middle and was immediately sorry because it meant having to buy a replacement. But what difference did it make? She and Tommy wouldn't live there much longer to be worried about a broken dish. Would they?

Later, she lay beside Frank and listened to the chirping of the crickets and the occasional whir of a plane engine in the clear, night sky. It had been on nights like this, sultry and starry-skyed that she had given herself, body and soul, to Peter.

From the very beginning of her stay at Aunt Jenny's summer home, Pete captivated her. She met the two Wakeland brothers the summer she visited her aunt after her senior year ended in New Orleans. She found Frank, the eldest, to be somewhat ill-mannered and sloppily dressed. She also resented how his dark gaze followed her every movement when she trailed after her aunt to the Wakeland farm to collect the rent. However, it was the blond-haired Pete with the impeccable manners and the passion to learn who impressed her. He'd secretly pursued her, and she reciprocated his interest, not prepared for the glorious feelings he aroused in her.

She fell deeply in love with Pete, giving all of herself to him, holding nothing back. However, Pete was extremely serious, sparse with words as well as feelings. During one of their nights together under the stars, he surprised her by confiding his desire to be a surgeon.

"I've got a gift, Ellie. Working as an orderly in that two-bit hospital in town has shown me what I need to do in life. I feel it inside of me." He tapped his chest with his index finger. "I can contribute to the world, and no one is going to stand in my way. Not even you."

"Me? How could I do that?"

"Forget it. I didn't mean it."

"Tell me. I have a right to know what you think."

"You have no rights to my thoughts!" His blue eyes hardened and gleamed like marbles in the moonlight, so unlike the soft, brown ones of his brother. "I don't mean to hurt your feelings, but you just get under my skin sometimes because you've never had to work for anything or want for anything."

"I can't help it if my people have some money. I resent being condemned for it." She released herself from his loose embrace and sat up, a lump forming in her throat.

Pete sighed and pulled himself up from his reclining position. "Don't pout, Ellie. You're acting like a spoiled little girl. Just because you're related to a big shot family in this parish, you think you can have whatever you want. And you want me."

"Suppose I do want you?" she shot back. "What's wrong with that? I love you. If you want to be a doctor, I won't stand in your way. I'll even ask Aunt Jenny to lend you the money for medical school. She thinks you're meant for greater things than farming."

She'd have offered Pete her aunt's entire estate if it would insure his love.

Pete stood and blocked out the light from the moon. "There is no way I will ever accept help from your aunt. My father worked his tail off for her all of his life and was barely forty years old when he died because he was worn out. And now Frank is doing the same thing. And what does my brother get for all of this but a rented piece of land and the 'privilege' of farming for your aunt?"

Bending down, Pete scooped up a clump of dirt and held it out for her to see. "This is what killed my dad, and it will kill my brother, but it won't kill me!"

He flung the dirt against an oak tree.

Ellie quickly rose to her feet, eager to calm him yet distressed and unnerved by his outburst, something she'd never before seen. She placed her hand gently on his arm, and she looked at him in the moonlight before his lips brushed her cheek.

"I don't want you to get in trouble, Ellie. You better head on home before your aunt comes looking for you. I'm sorry I exploded. This isn't like me."

"I love you, Pete, and I always will."

Pete smiled and left her standing alone.

Not long afterwards he disappeared from her life. He left her a short note, telling her he had no choice, he must leave and pursue his dream. No mention of love, yet she believed with all of her heart, he would return for her.

After long days of waiting with no further word from him, she grew furious with herself and with Peter Wakeland. She felt he had used her, and she vowed to make him sorry.

Within a month, she married his handsome, older brother.

Barely eight months later, she bore a son prematurely, and she was never certain who was the father, and actually she didn't want to know. Frank, however, accepted Tommy as his own.

Their marriage was far from idyllic. Frank could be coarse and crude at times, but Ellie accepted his failings because she knew he loved her and Tommy, and because she had nowhere else to go.

Aunt Jenny disinherited her after her elopement and bequeathed all of the money to charity. The historic, old home was turned into a museum, operated by the state. The only other thing that held her marriage together was her powerful attraction to Frank. She responded to him in spite of herself, and this made her feel unfaithful to Pete.

She quietly left their bed, careful not to wake Frank and walked to the bureau. Rummaging beneath her underwear, she found Pete's note and pressed it to her chest. The very feel of the paper made her feel closer to him as it had done all through her marriage.

"If he asks you, are you goin' to leave?"

Ellie jumped at the sound of Frank's voice in the darkness.

He switched on the bedside lamp. "You look ridiculous, Ellie, just like some lovestruck heroine in one of those books you're always readin'. Don't look surprised. I've known about that letter for years. I may be slow in learnin' book things but in common sense, I got it all over Pete. He was the stupid one for lettin' you go."

"Pete's a wonderful doctor. Don't call him stupid."

Ellie gave Frank a scathing look, but her cheeks burned with humiliation to realize he knew about the letter.

Frank shrugged and calmly lit a cigarette. "Sure, he's a good doctor, and he's saved lives, but he broke your heart, and he can't sew it back again. But I did. Or I thought I had."

Ellie placed the letter beneath her silk slip in the drawer, unable to think of anything to say to Frank. Sitting on the rose printed sheets on her side of the bed, she stared at the wall. Part of her wanted him to be a little jealous for keeping Pete's note.

After a few minutes of awkward silence between them, Frank extinguished his cigarette in the ashtray. "You haven't answered my question, Honey. Would you go with Pete if he asked you?"

A strangled sigh escaped her at the absurdity of the situation. "I really don't know. Until this minute, I thought I knew, but now after all of this time..."

Her voice became a whisper, "I'm not sure what I'll do when the time comes, if it comes. Please believe I don't want to hurt you."

Frank pulled her against him and whispered against her hair, "Maybe this will help you decide."

Oh, she knew where this was headed!

"Frank, this isn't fair." She felt herself succumbing to his kisses and hated herself for her weakness.

"Love is all I've got, Ellie."

Looking into his face, she saw the passion she'd seen hundreds of times before, but caught up in her dream world, she'd not comprehended the love or the hurt he must have quietly harbored because of Pete's note. He'd given himself totally to her since the day they married, and she now realized she had given nothing in return. As she looked into his soft, brown eyes, so unlike his brother's, she knew Frank loved her enough to free her if she wished it, and she could ask for nothing more.

* * * * *

Ellie watched Pete's Cadillac disappear in a cloud of dust down the road.

His visit had lasted a few hours and most of his time had been spent with Frank and Tommy, discussing his busy life and the price of beans.

He'd spent a few minutes with her, commenting on how wonderful the house looked and what good care she took of her family and how beautiful she still was and then he left.

She realized he was a busy man, living to save lives with little time for himself or a family of his own. For Pete, the past was over, and she along with it. She didn't exist for him; perhaps she never had.

Frank waved one final time and looked at her with his dark, probing gaze. "I reckon you'll never know the answer to that question now, will you, Ellie?"

She touched his hand and felt his fingers curl around her own.

"I know the answer," she said and stood on tip-toe to kiss his lips. "I know the answer very well."

The End

First published in *Ellipsis*, Vol.8, No.1, University of New Orleans, 1980.

Mirrors of the Soul

The doorbell rings. I hobble to it, leaning upon my cane for support. The cortisone has eased my arthritis, and I am better able to maneuver my way across the length of the house. I open the door to see a pretty, young woman, casually dressed in a pullover sweater and jeans.

"Are you Mrs. Morelli who has the room for rent?" she asks.

"Yes."

"Hi, I'm Janice Grant. I saw your ad in the college newspaper for a boarder. Have you rented the room yet?"

I notice her eyes are a vivid shade of blue, but that isn't what holds my attention. I see something behind the eyes, something I can't comprehend.

"No, the room is still available," I tell her. "Would you care to see it?" Part of me wants to say the room is rented, but no one else has answered the ad. We need the extra money from a boarder since Oliver didn't receive an expected raise last semester.

I unlock the screen door. She pulls it open and hesitantly walks into the foyer, her eyes large and probing as she gazes at the staircase and the parlor beyond the doorway. I catch a whiff of her perfume, a floral fragrance which I don't like.

Tossing her long blonde hair, she smiles a smile which crinkles the corners of her eyes. "Oh, I like your house. It's so lovely. Have you lived here long?"

"All of my life. My grandparents owned it."

"How wonderful to have grown up in such an enchanting place. I grew up in a small house outside of Natchez. Nothing as grand as this one."

"The room is upstairs. Third door on the left. I'd show it to you, but I'm not able to make it up the stairs very well."

She glances at my cane and my legs. I feel withered and old beneath her vibrant stare though I'm barely forty-eight.

"I understand, Mrs. Morelli. I'll find it."

Gracefully, she climbs the stairs and disappears.

I hear her footsteps above me as she enters the room. Small chills slither down my backside when I go into the kitchen to pour a cup of hot tea. A few minutes later, I return to the foyer to find her waiting on the bottom step.

"The room is perfect," she gushes, her eyes glowing with pleasure. "It's everything I'd hoped and so close to the campus. Are you related to Professor Morelli?"

"He's my husband."

"Oh, I've registered for his Historical Research class this semester. I'm a graduate student." She looks me straight in the eye with a half-smile on her lips when another chill creeps down my spine. "I would love to rent the room."

There is no reason not to rent it to her, but I hesitate a few seconds longer than necessary. I agree only so Oliver can sleep at night instead of worrying about bills.

"No smoking in the house," I warn her. "If you wish, you can pay extra and have your meals with us."

"Thank you so much, Ma'am. That sounds fine."

* * * * *

That evening Oliver drags himself through the front door.

Where is the buoyant step of the man I married, and where is his endless energy? I've failed this man who is my reason for living. I sigh and offer my face for his evening kiss.

I smell the familiar scent of pipe tobacco as he pecks the air in greeting and goes through the bills on the foyer table.

"I have some good news," I tell him.

"Hmmm," his deep voice responds, but he isn't paying attention. He seems more interested in the rate increase on the utility bill.

"I rented the room today to a graduate student named Janice Grant who's in one of your classes. She's moving in tomorrow."

He doesn't immediately reply, so I repeat myself.

Oliver looks up and tosses the bill onto the table. "I heard you, Viola."

"I'm not thrilled about having a stranger in the house, but we can use the extra money." As I move towards the parlor, he grabs my arm.

44

His handsome face contorts into a scowl. "You don't think I'm capable of providing for us, do you? You still regret my decision not to work for your father and his precious export company. I've done the best I can for us over the years. And now you've placed an ad in the college newspaper and gotten a paying boarder like we're paupers. It's embarrassing. *She* would never have done that."

"We need the extra money. I did this for you...for us." My heart feels like it's caught between a vise. Why has he mentioned *her* now after all of this time?

A look of repentance crosses his face, and he drops his hand. "I'm sorry. Guess I'm overtired. First day of the semester, you know." He rubs his temples with his index fingers. "I appreciate your making things easier for me."

Walking near the stairs, he abruptly stops and sniffs the air. "What's that scent I've been smelling since I came in the door?"

I wrinkle my nose in distaste. "Our new boarder apparently doused herself with the perfume bottle."

"I like it. Smells like roses after a summer's rain."

Oliver whistles and heads upstairs.

I freeze, rooted to the floor. I recognize that tune he whistles, a tune he hasn't whistled in many years. *It was their song, his and hers.* And then it hits me like a storm from the Gulf--that scent Janice Grant wore is the same scent *she* wore so long ago. *Delia, my sister.*

* * * * *

Janice has been in the house one month and has totally captivated Oliver. She is quite friendly to him but speaks little to me. In the mornings they leave together for the small, private college where Oliver teaches, their chatter echoing across the lawn and out the gate to the street. The spring is back in Oliver's step, the tired lines erased from his face.

Once, I was energetic and considered pretty though not as beautiful or vivacious as Delia. During her freshman year at the college, she had her choice of any rich, handsome young man on campus. But she chose poor, hardworking Oliver, the man on whom I set my sophomoric heart. Unhappily for me, he reciprocated her interest.

45

I felt Oliver was destined for greater things than a teaching career, but Delia dazzled him with her beauty and her support of whatever he wanted to do in life. He told me she would be the perfect wife for him, but I couldn't bear the thought of Oliver marrying my sister.

I remained silent, believing the infatuation would wane.

It didn't.

The month before their wedding, I found her sitting by her desk in her bedroom, scribbling notes of appreciation for the incoming wedding gifts. I sat upon her bed and fingered an embroidered rosette on the spread.

"Oliver isn't meant for you. He should be marrying me. You stole him from me, and you will never be happy; he will not be happy because you're not right for him."

Delia's pen ceased moving, and she turned her dark gaze upon me. "Viola, I didn't steal Oliver from you. His heart never belonged to you in the first place. I'm sorry for your pain, but you must get over this obsession."

She patted my hand in a placating gesture, but I pulled away. I looked levelly at her, always feeling she could see within my soul with those dancing brown eyes of hers, and right then, I knew she could.

I riveted my attention upon Oliver's photograph on her dresser. "I love him and I will have him, someway I will."

I had no clue why I said such a thing since I had no plan in my mind, no plan at all. Just empty words spoken in the heat of unbearable heart ache.

Leaving her room, I reached the landing at the top of the stairs, not certain what to do. For an instant I even considered flinging myself down the long, wide staircase, a broken heap on the floor for my parents to find. Would Oliver even care? The thought fled when I heard Delia's voice behind me.

"Viola, please forgive me if I've hurt you. I love you."

I turned on her, my voice rising to the rafters. "You've never loved anyone but yourself. Always Mother's and Daddy's little pet. Always getting the attention because of how pretty you are, how sweet, how smart, always getting what you want; and I get the leftovers because I'm older, the responsible one. I'm sick of it!"

"Viola, I'm sorry. I truly am!" Her hand grazed my back.

"Don't touch me!"

Whirling away, I attempted to rush down the stairs when Delia moved at the same second and stumbled. She grabbed at the banister but missed. Horrified, I watched her topple headlong down the steep steps. The thumping sound of her head as she hit the marble stairs will echo within my brain for the rest of my life. But time passes and life continues even where tragedies occur.

Oliver later married me because I am the next best thing to my sister. I live with this knowledge because Oliver is my life.

* * * * *

I sit in the kitchen when Oliver and Janice return from the college. I observe them without being noticed. She seems absorbed by a page he shows her in a textbook. She giggles, he laughs and lights his pipe.

They spot me and come to where I sit. Oliver kisses me on the forehead while Janice murmurs a polite hello. Her azure gaze examines me, seeming to search my soul and unnerves me.

"Viola, you'll never guess what Professor Jordan has Janice researching for Philosophy. Reincarnation."

Oliver pours them both a cup of tea.

I lift my shoulders in disinterest, but Oliver and Janice begin a lively discussion on the subject.

"Many people do believe in it, Oliver. Could explain why certain people like one another or hate each other because they were either friends or enemies in former lifetimes. It's also believed some souls reincarnate into the same family groups. It seems logical to me."

"Interesting, but I'm not a believer in the occult," Oliver admits.

"Neither am I," I say.

I sense her gaze bores holes into my back when I leave the kitchen. *I've also noticed her familiar use of Oliver's first name.*

That night, the Grandfather clock strikes twelve in the foyer. I lie in my bed in the spare bedroom and listen to the house settle. I've learned to sleep alone. Oliver prefers to sleep in the upstairs bedroom we once shared. He hasn't approached me in more than two years, not since it became too painful for me to climb the stairs. However, our couplings over the years were few-

and-far between as Delia's memory always seemed to intrude. Even in death, she triumphs.

My bedroom is directly below Oliver's. I hear a door shut and the patter of feet across the floor. Soft, intimate giggles float through the ceiling. Then the endless creaking of the bed springs. I place my hands over my ears and tightly close my eyes as tears slip down my face.

* * * * *

I am seated by the kitchen table when they come down to breakfast. How civil we are. My husband eats his eggs, and his mistress swallows the coffee and biscuits I prepared. They make small talk, and Oliver tries to include me, but I sit quietly. My brain is feverish with thoughts of them despite my seeming calm. This is my home and my husband, but I am once again the outsider. Another young woman has captured my Oliver's heart. I imagine Delia with Oliver, Janice with Oliver.

Those bright blue eyes, bluer than the ocean, intently watch me. I look deeply into them, and whether it's from lack of sleep or the conversation about reincarnation the previous day, a shock of recognition streaks through me, and *I know.*

"Delia!" I'm unable to control myself. I tremble so hard my teeth chatter. I point an accusing finger at Janice. "She's back, Oliver! She's reborn!"

Oliver not only looks confused but frightened, especially when I shout it again. He pushes back his chair and clutches my shoulders. "Viola, calm down. Are you having another breakdown?"

How dare he mention the mental breakdown I suffered after a miscarriage twenty years ago! We agreed never to speak of it.

Oliver nods to Janice. "Jan, go on ahead to class."

"Can I help?"

"No, I need to settle her down."

He picks me up and carries me to my bedroom. I flail against him as he places me on the bed. I catch a glimpse of myself in the cheval mirror. My hair is disheveled, my eyes wild and fevered, my face as white as the sheets. I look every inch the mad woman.

Sitting beside me, he clasps my hand, more like a father than a husband. "Have you forgotten to take your medication? Shall I call your doctor?"

I grab at his shirt. "I'm okay! No doctor!"

He looks unconvinced. "I haven't seen you this incoherent or worked up in a long time."

What a jerk he can sometimes be! I rear back, unable to remain quiet a minute longer. "Shouldn't I be worked up, upset when my husband sleeps with another woman in my very own house? In the room above my head? Do you think I'm deaf as well as stupid?"

He slowly stands, thrusts his hands in his pockets and breathes a long sigh. "I beg your forgiveness, Viola, I do. I knew it was wrong. Not an excuse, but nothing has been the same for me since Delia died. Jan makes me feel alive again and reminds me of her."

Glancing out of the window, he then turns with such a dismal look on his face that I wish to scream. "I won't leave you. You've been a good wife to me. And I'm too old to start over again. I've decided to break off with her."

"Don't do me any favors! I should kick your cheating behind to the curb!" My heart breaks to once again be Oliver's consolation prize.

"I wouldn't blame you if you did."

Leaning over me, he pecks my forehead and tells me to rest. He then assures me he will be home early so we can talk. After he's gone, I finger where his lips touched me, and I wonder why my skin hasn't eroded from the many years of his empty kisses.

* * * * *

Later, as I recline on the bed, curiosity about Janice gnaws at me. There is nothing about her I can label as distinctly Delia, but I decide I must know more. Painfully and carefully, I trod up the stairs like a toddler.

The bedroom no longer retains remnants of Delia. The furnishings and drapes were changed years ago. Janice has added some photos of her family members and a painting of a mansion in Natchez to the wall, and on the nightstand are some paperback novels. Perfume bottles and makeup tubes litter the dressing table. Her clothes neatly hang in the closet. Nothing here but Janice Grant, nothing of Delia. I'm a foolish woman, thinking absurd thoughts. Oliver's affair has rattled me. I close the door and walk to the landing where I'm startled to see Janice with red-rimmed eyes and tear-streaked cheeks.

I surmise Oliver has broken off with her.

"Pack your things and be out of my house by tonight."

"Oliver said you know about us."

"Hard not to know with such a noisy bed."

"I love him, but I'm leaving only because he won't abandon you."

"I'm his wife. What did you expect he'd do?"

"Leave to have a life with *me*. I've never felt this way about anyone, but I love him enough to respect his wishes. Our souls are connected...forever."

Her words and attitude distress me. I must get away from her. Limping past her, I remember playing a similar scenario on these very same stairs with Delia.

"I want you gone," I insist, hovering on the edge of a panic attack and unable to catch a deep breath.

Janice stands closer to the wall, silent, unmoving, almost unseeing, as if she's somehow fallen into a hypnotic trance. *Is she remembering, too?*

I position myself on the top stair while I cling to the banister. I toddle down one step when a sharp pain claws at my heart. The pain is so intense that I drop my cane and clutch my chest with both hands. I sway off balance then feel myself falling forward. Hitting each cool, marble step, I tumble towards the floor, screaming the entire way until thick darkness descends and stifles my screams.

* * * * *

Warm and swaddled within my blanket, I open my eyes, squinching from the glare of the fluorescent lights above me. Someone wheels me along the hospital corridor where I hear hungry, demanding cries. I'm a bit apprehensive since The-Powers-That-Be informed me I shall totally forget once I sleep. *I don't wish to forget*, but already Viola's memories are fading.

A nurse asks, "What is the name?"

A feminine voice answers, "Anna Maria Morelli."

I am lifted from the crib to see a man, dressed in a yellow hospital gown. He grins as the nurse hands me to the beaming blonde-haired woman in the hospital bed.

He bends over us. "Such a beautiful baby, sweetheart. Looks like you. I'm glad we named her after my mother."

"She's a perfect, healthy baby in every way. We've been blessed."

"You know, I'm going to spoil our little princess. She'll be a daddy's girl for certain."

My mother's fingers stroke my cheek. She looks directly into my eyes, and I stare into her ocean-blue ones, both of us locked in a moment of knowing.

Her gaze darkens, and she pushes me into my father's arms. "Take her, Oliver!"

"Jan, what's wrong?"

She makes no reply. I feel the protective warmth of my father's body against mine, already knowing he loves me. I coo my contentment, close my eyes, and fall asleep to soon wake into forgetfulness.

The End

Black and White and Red All Over

By: Michael Verrett

I've got lots of time to talk about dreams or any subject for that matter. My status is well, – limbo.

Why?

You see, two nights earlier, I witnessed something.

I'll eventually get around to telling the gory details, but something else happened. Which brings to why I'm stuck in this eternal monologue.

I'm in an induced trance.

The police hypnotist's name is Stan. I later learned he's a friend of the chief of police. I didn't know Stan had decided to invite himself into the murder investigation. I was supposed to meet with the police sketch artist. His name is Robert. Anyway, that's how I ended up in a dark room with Stan the hypnotist.

After his little tricks-of-the-trade, I now find myself in a state called true somnambulism. Perfect rest both mentally, physically, and – prone to giggle.

I have no idea of my physical position on his official couch. I don't know if my skirt is hiked up or my legs too far apart. I have no concept of time.

My memory returned to the murder. There's an old joke – what's black and white and read/red all over. Red and read being homonyms. So, what's read/red and white and black all over? The answer is a newspaper. My recollection of the murder is the same except the operative word is "red" and *not* "read."

The interior of the killer's car was illuminated with the vehicle's dome light. With rain falling and the external gloom, the killer's face and that of the victim's appeared as a grainy black and white. His mouth and her eyes were brilliant red.

After talking with high-testosterone uniform officers and then the detectives, oh, and I forgot to mention avoiding the TV media, the police set me up to do a sketch – a police sketch.

It would take a couple of days because Robert was off, and this was of some concern and angst to the detective. The chief of police decided they were cutting back on overtime pay. That meant the detectives could not set up the sketch until he returned to work.

Seems the detectives and the uniform officers didn't think too highly of Chief Arglane.

They grumbled about his decisions, considered his positions on law enforcement too limp-wristed, and his speeches and proclamations, evidence of depleted chromosomes. Who would ever think the petty actions of an appointed bureaucrat would have a dramatic impact on your life?

So, I would have to wait to meet this sketch artist when it was convenient for the chief of police and not the integrity of the investigation.

I have to point out I'm quoting the detective on this as well as the comment about depleted chromosomes.

Since then, my dreams torment me. It's as if the killer somehow slipped out of the real world and into my subconscious. He haunts and hunts me in my dreams.

So, pardon me while I extemporize once again.

My dreams were once my own. I dreamed in shades of ordinary anxiety. My version of things that go bump in the night were experiences shared by other women. Everyday frustrations. Forgetting little and big things, missing deadlines, the mishaps that trip us up.

Then there were the bizarre forays. The one *sans* clothing. Who can deny ever having the embarrassing and confusing where-are-my-clothes dreams? Sometimes complete nudity while other times missing those important articles. My exposure was always attended by real and imaginary compatriots, none of them interested in the least that my subconscious paraded me about in my birthday suit.

Then there were the odd ones. Being in strange hotel rooms surrounded by people that I supposedly knew, all the while trying to reconcile my luggage. The curious thing was that, although I was keenly aware of my state of exposure, the other characters floating about in my nocturnal soup seemed indifferent.

A frequent dream occurred as I traveled by air.

These exacerbating dreams were a jumble of jostled timetables, the irritation of losing touch with family or traveling companion, and the exasperation of misplacing my ticket.

If you think I am rambling – you are correct. I prefer rambling rather than a real-life nightmare. Like Mrs. McGillicuddy in Agatha Christie's, *4:50 From Paddington,* I witnessed a murder. I saw the killer's face.

Unlike Christie's redoubtable septuagenarian, Mrs. Marple, I did not become a force of nature, badgering reluctant and feckless police, all the while pursuing clues to the point of reckless, personal danger.

While I had always thought...hoped...assumed I had that sort of grit, alas, I instead have spiraled toward the opposite end of the spectrum. My plucky courage was all but slack. My sails depleted for want of a following breeze.

That night, I stumbled with a stack of packages and purchases into the rainy evening in search of my new SUV. It was all due to a favor. A favor for a friend. Her name's Sally.

Sally was in charge of collecting and storing the trimming for the very-pregnant Olivia's big reveal party. We, her co-workers, had all chipped-in for cake, balloons, and bubbly.

"Olivia."

I just love her name; I love the classical names. Mine's "Emma" and it is also very classy and classical–but I digress.

The bottom line was Sally couldn't pick up the party stuff. It had to be that day because the place was closed the next day due to Labor Day. She called me, and since I'm the dependable and reliable kind, also known as a sucker, I said, "Of course."

So, I get to Landry's Cake Emporium, and the cake was one color, and the balloons, that Miss Gladys, the sales lady, was trying to push on me, did not match.

How much common sense does it take to realize if the cake had blue icing, the balloons shouldn't be PINK! I insisted on blue balloons. Then she gave me this nonsense that blue balloons were more expensive because they were bigger! And it was going to cost me $10 for blue. Then I did a spellcheck on the icing. Congratulations, "It's a Buy!"

Did I mention Gladys was not a proficient agent of the English language?

"No, Gladys," I said, "'Boy' is misspelled."

"It looks like a 'B'," said Gladys.

"Gladys," I said with restraint, "it's the *vowel* that's misspelled – not the consonants. It's a boy, 'B O Y' not a 'B U Y'."

"Well, so it is; you know, it's not a big deal. It's not like the little fellow can read. He's not going to notice the mistake."

"Gladys," I said with a slight edge in my voice, "I know he can't read. He hasn't been born yet. And his mommy is not teaching him braille in the womb. Fix it!"

"No problem," said Gladys. "I'll have Kenny in the back change the 'U' into an 'O'."

"I'll wait."

How long can it take to drop a dot of blue turning a 'U' into an 'O'?

Only twenty-five minutes. I'm telling you now, there were nearly three murders that night! One in the parking lot and two in the store. Gladys and Kenny were that close to being found in the freezer by the day shift.

Gladys eventually handed me the cake, the blue balloons, and surprise – extra boxes. Extra stuff that Sally and the others had purchased which I never knew about. Cupcakes? Why buy *cupcakes* if you have a *cake*? Party favors that are shaped like tiny little male... never mind, I'm tired of repeating this part.

Curtain fell. Raindrops the size of 'gummy bears' formed a gauntlet between me and my SUV; I'd parked on the other side of planet Mars.

I pulled up my collar and ventured out into a world of motors, squealing tires and glaring headlights. A car driving too fast splashed a water puddle. Chilling water sloshed up my legs.

The leaning-tower-of-packages had me ambling about like a wino.

As I approached my new car, I saw that some jackass in an orange van had parked over the painted line at an angle with his front wheels near my bumper.

Stopping at the trunk, I hit the keypad. The trunk opened majestically. I dumped the packages in the back except for the cake. Big Blue was getting a ride next to me on the front seat.

I opened the front passenger door and strapped the cake down like it was an astronaut headed for space.

That's when I first heard moaning.

I looked around; there was nothing but traffic and the distant, flickering lights of the stores and traffic signals.

The rain was slackening as I tried to squeeze between the van and my vehicle. There was enough room to open the door, and if I could think thin enough and take off my coat, I'd be able to make it.

With the door open, I removed my coat and tossed it in along with my purse. That's when I realized just how close the passenger window was to my door. With keys in hand, I inched into the narrow space. The wet metal of my vehicle leaked through my clothes, chilling and soaking me. In the window of the van was a face. A woman's face.

Blonde hair.

She seemed to be trying to say something.

I shouldn't have looked.

Next to her was a brute of a man. Low forehead, deep-set eyes and a leering grin. He was strangling the blonde. He ripped her blouse open exposing her bra and then breasts. His massive hands squeezed her neck, then released. Squeezed and released. Her eyes rolled back in her head. Her tongue leapt about. She frantically pawed the window with her left hand.

This man, this creature, stared at me the whole time. His leer became a laugh as the whole of his body thrusted against her until his head banged against the window glass.

I hurried to get inside my vehicle. My keys fell. I squeezed through the driver's door and felt about for the keys.

Not thinking, I could have started my vehicle, but I panicked.

My fingers kept reaching and searching. When the latch on the van's passenger door clicked, it was then I remembered I could drive away or at least some distance *without* the key.

The engine roared to life, and I hit the gas.

Through my rear-view mirror, I watched.

Rain droplets partially obscured the view, but I saw his exit, dragging her body by her hair with one hand. He wore a T-shirt and was barrel chested. As big a man I had ever seen, he was also naked from the waist down.

Not wanting my engine to quit, I made a circle, turned on my lights and started honking my horn. He clambered back into the van and drove away, leaving the dead woman.

I sped up and aimed my SUV at the business, then dropped it into neutral.

The engine died, but there was enough momentum to dodge traffic and pull onto the sidewalk where I stopped.

Pulling out my phone, I dialed #911.

My hands trembled, and I desperately needed the bathroom. I went inside and walked right past Gladys and a sign that read Employees Only.

"You can't go in there!" protested Gladys, "that's for the boy employees!"

"You mean the 'buy' employees," I corrected her.

The 911 Operator finally answered. "911, what's your emergency?"

Now I had *two* emergencies. One was a murdered woman, and the other was Kenny who occupied the only stall.

"911, what's your emergency?" she repeated.

Holding the phone with my chin, I overwhelmed her with information.

Standing at the urinal with both hands free, I forced down my underwear and hiked up my dress. I proceeded to multitask in a way I had never tried before.

Then Kenny, from within the stall, engaged me. "Is somebody there?"

"Stay in there, Kenny," I said. "It's for your own good. And when I tell you to come out, bring some toilet paper."

"Mom? Is that you?" he asked.

First, the uniform officers arrived.

The last place you should ever want to commit a crime is in the vicinity of a bakery that gives cops coffee and donuts for half price.

Seeing the police, Gladys went apoplectic. "I fixed it," she said frantically to the officer. "She didn't have to buy the 'Buy'. The 'U'. I had it fixed with an 'O.' Don't put me in jail. It was Kenny."

"What is she talking about?" Officer McClin asked.

"Wheel of Fortune," I said to the officer. "You know, Pat and Vanna."

"Oh, okay."

He took my statement while a host of officers with blue flashing lights surrounded the body in the parking lot.

A cute cop brought me my keys. "McClin said to look for car keys. Said they belonged to the witness. My name's Harry."

"He told you using 'ESP'?"

"No, Ma'am, not the sports channel, the police radio."

He stood there, rocking on his heels with his thumbs tucked into his pistol belt, waiting, no doubt, for his next witty line to formulate.

Meanwhile, I checked out his holstered gun.

What would I have done if I had had a gun? Probably shot myself in the toe.

"Harry, beat it."

The deep voice snapped me out of my James Bond, John Wayne mindset. The voice belonged to a big guy who looked sharp in a gray suit and a dazzling blue tie. While Harry was cute, this man was different. There was a *vibe* about him.

"Ms. Harris," he said, scribbling on his notepad. "I'm Detective Scott. I work homicide. I'd like for you to come down to our office where we can get a statement. Is there anything you need to do or anything that would keep that from happening?"

We went to his office where I repeated what I'd said to the uniform officers. I drove home knowing that I'd have to wait for the call from the one giving me date and time to meet the police sketch artist and possibly reacquaint myself with Detective Scott.

That was the end of the big night.

So, now you know as much as the police knew. What I didn't know was that the police had an idea who the murderer might be. Had I known that, my nights may have been more peaceful.

That first night, I went to bed as usual. I took a little pill, but it failed to live up to its promised effect. I stared up at the slow rotation of the ceiling fan. When sleep finally found me, the dreams kicked into high gear. The first involved my applying for a secretarial position with Detective Scott and a host of other police officers. In the dream, I was to demonstrate my typing skills.

Confusion began when my size changed. The chair suddenly became three times as large.

There was a chair and desk. I removed my bright teal jacket and took a seat before a large computer and keyboard. I began typing the quick brown fox and realized it was one of those *sans* clothing dreams. I wore nothing beneath my jacket. Realizing my predicament, I reached for my jacket, but it had disappeared. I got on my hands and knees and searched around the chair and beneath the desk to no avail.

Then the color schemes disappeared. The dream faded to black and white. He was here. The killer was interloping. I closed my eyes. His hot breath found my neck. He whispered names, women's names, as if trying to either guess mine or trick me into admitting it was me.

I crawled across the floor constricted by a tight skirt. I heard him laughing. I peeked and saw a large pair of dirty jeans in my path. Avoiding them, I crawled and came upon the body of the dead woman, lying on the floor and facing away from me. I was trapped – blocked under the desk by her body. My own body suddenly changed and grew twice its size. I was topless and now squeezed beneath the desk by my own volume.

Then I felt a hand tug my ankle....

I awoke.

"That's the last time I'm taking that pill," I said to no one.

The next day was Labor Day.

I remained home and slouched. I called Sally and begged her to come and get the stuff for the reveal party. I was not in the mood for company, but I couldn't be rude to Sally.

When she arrived, I feigned a headache. The comment went in one ear and out of the other.

"Did you hear about the woman being murdered outside Landry's Cake Emporium? My God, Emma, it could have been *me* if I'd picked up the cake."

"Yeah, Sally," I said, "but it wasn't."

"What about that poor, dead girl? The police aren't saying much, but I suspect she was a redhead and probably a stripper – don't you think?"

"I suspect she was blonde and possibly a meteorologist. She was probably giving him the weather." I tried really hard at being cynical. This, too, went in one ear and out the other.

"More likely giving him a lap leaner, and he got mad because it wasn't happening," said Sally.

Okay, I said to myself. Sally has got to go.

"Sally, I didn't sleep well yesterday, uh, last night, and ohhhh!" I faked an exaggerated yawn. "I think it's catching up with me."

"Do you want me to go? I'll go if you just say the word."

"Sally, go."

"Sure thing. I mean you need your sleep. God, you look something awful. I'll just be going."

"Thanks for being understanding."

After Sally left, I returned to the couch and promptly fell asleep.

This time he was waiting for me. He wore the dirty jeans and nothing else. His paw of a hand seized me by the neck as he forced my lips upon his. There was a taste like fish oil. His tongue pushed against my gritting teeth.

For some reason, I thought of Alice – of all things, 'Alice in Wonderland'. I escaped his grip by falling into the rabbit hole. Above, he stomped and cursed reminding me of a rampaging giant. I expected to find the Eat-Me cake and Drink-Me bottle. Alas, the Alice theme quickly evaporated.

It was replaced by another childhood story.

Wendy was reading to her younger brothers. I was in the room and knew that Peter Pan had to be skulking around. I searched for him, but he was not to be found.

I knew I was safe here. Safe in my childhood memories. The killer could not get me here.

Colors returned as a purple, pastel sky, dotted with stars, arose. I counted one, then two. Two stars to the right and straight...

I awoke at my house.

The call came the next day. The meeting with the sketch artist was set for four in the afternoon.

That night in my bedroom, I slept with the lights on. There was a Cary Grant movie on television, and it was scheduled for two hours. I nodded off just as he and Sophia Loren were hitting it off.

I slept peacefully for an hour.

The sound of stormy weather awakened me. On the TV screen, the picture was black and white. The killer was near.

With the remote control, I searched the channel guide. Then the power went out. I recited quotes from 'Alice in Wonderland'.

Nothing happened.

A dresser drawer opened. He went through my night things. Pulling them out and tossing them on the floor. Next, he moved to my underthings. He made growling sounds and sniffed like a dog.

I pulled the covers over my head in the hopes he would tire of this game and go. His weight impacted the bed. The sound of his unfastening zipper let me know he was undressing. I thought again about the police officer's gun. What if I had it? Would I shoot holes in my house in the expectation that bullets would work on a demon?

Then came the odor again. The fish oil odor. It seemed he sat on his knees over me. The protecting covers responded as touches and rough shoves impacted the sympathetic material.

His hands fondled me through the bedding.

"Go away or else," I said even as my voice faded.

"Or else what?" He laughed. "Touch me where I tell you to touch me."

"Go, or...I'll tell...I'll tell...the Queen of Hearts."

"Touch me."

"Hah!" I said. "You can't touch me. I'm hiding amongst my childhood books. You best beware the Queen of Hearts. She is childish, foul-tempered, and acts with blind fury."

"Touch me," he repeated over and over.

The heat beneath the cover increased rapidly. The air became unbearable. I couldn't take it any longer.

I sat straight up.

The dream had ended.

So, now we are up to date with my story. I wait for Stan to get on with it when the door opens and the lights come on. Detective Scott and Stan argue.

You had no permission to hypnotize the witness," said Scott.

"Chief Arglane gave me permission," said Stan.

"He's not in charge of this investigation," said Detective Scott. "Now, get out!"

"Hypnosis is not required for a sketch, Stan." It was the sketch artist speaking. "The cognitive interview method I employ has demonstrated the memory can be improved five-fold over what hypnosis can accomplish."

I'm not sure what happened, but a fight broke out amongst the police detectives. I later learned Detective Scott was suspended by the chief, and Stan went to the hospital with a broken nose and eye socket.

The fight went from the desk to the floor. I laughed and giggled as the two men tumbled near me. Scott gave Stan three good socks to the face and that was that. The sketch artist was able to bring me out of the trance.

I awoke to see Detective Scott dragging Stan out of the door and leaving him unconscious in the hallway.

Three hours later, the sketch was complete. "What do you think?" the artist asked Scott.

"That's going to be him," said Scott. "The state police should have never hired the guy in the first place."

Scott pulled a photo out of his pocket and showed it to the artist. "The only photo we had was ten years old when the state finally fired him. Didn't want to show it to the witness on account we weren't sure, and the age of the picture doesn't do him...justice."

"You know who the killer is?" I asked.

"Yeah, but he's going to be hard to recognize," said the artist.

"You heard already?" said Scott. "Shame we couldn't have gotten a warrant for him sooner. Would have saved a life and he'd have gotten picked up earlier when the uniform guys spotted his van on Ocean Drive."

"What are you talking about?"

"If we could have gotten the sketch done earlier, we'd have been able to convince a judge to sign a search warrant giving us access to more recent photos. Then we would have put together a photo line-up for you to view, and once you'd picked him out, we'd have gotten a warrant for his arrest. Instead, he continued his crime spree until earlier today."

"What happened today?" I asked.

"He murdered someone else," said Scott. "Started a chase. He and his van tried to beat the express train at the crossing on College Drive. He came in second place – not a good thing to happen with a train."

"Is he dead?" I asked.

"Very much so," said Scott. "Decapitated."

"Decapitated?"

"Yeah," said Scott. "Off with his head." He chuckled.

"What do you mean? Off with his head?"

"It's a line from 'Alice in Wonderland'," said Scott. "The train that killed him was the 'Red Queen Express'."

Poetry

By: Evelyn Marie (Lott) Sanders

Short Ode On Poetry

Poetry can be sung by others,
Or, Poetry can be spoken by another.

Poetry can be precise, alive with perfection,
Or, Poetry can stir imagination and passion.

Poetry can be strange and unassuming,
Or, Poetry can be soulfully fulfilling.

Poetry can shake up our memories,
Or, Poetry can become new and unfamiliar.

Poetry can be mystifying and elusive,
Or, Poetry can be awesomely creative.

Poetry may not be works of reality, logic or rigidity,
But, Poetry can inspire us to reflect on unveiled truths leading to harmony.

Evelyn Marie (Lott) Sanders

Wild Mountain Trail Ride

Had I but listened to my soul, or my mind,
Would have known, for sure...
Long in leg with a full flowing silvery mane,
The guide said, "he's ready for old age care!"

Climbing aboard, I'd ridden before, I patted his neck.
Clucking sounds passed my lips.
Heels gently tapped his pale sides.
Smoothly we passed through the gate.

Up so high, we could almost touch the sky,
Right onto a steep mountain trail,
Watched an eagle fly by.
What a great trip!

Mountain air, so fresh, so clean,
Tiny yellow meadow flowers on the scene.
Their scent so absolutely divine,
Never to imagine, I would want to scream!

Down went his nose into the cluster,
Pulling up those reins, I felt his muscles quiver.
Front legs in the air, hooves batting a nose,
Jumping on hind legs on that trail, it, a mere sliver.

Eyes moon-sized, mouth wide open, mine....
Bucking like a young bronc,and me, I'm groping,
Pullin' on reins, the pommel, his mane, anything
To hold on to, yelling, "Whoa, whoa, stop your yo, yo-ing!"

What's it gonna take to stop 'em?
Stirrups slapping his sides.....
Hold 'em out, so as not to hit them...
Please end this wild Mountain Ride.

Finally, one last hunched straight up bucking to go.
Sliding off, practically falling down on weak knees,
And me, wishing for a soft seat on a patio pillow,
"Aha," the guide said, "you're a one-woman rodeo show!"

A week of wilderness bow-hunting, camped in a tent,
Packed up everything, with panniers loaded, now ready to go,
Walked all the way down that steep mountain trail.....
Umph! Not ready for Social Security was that old palomino!

A True Mountain Trail Ride in Colorado

Evelyn Marie (Lott) Sanders

Beyond Belief

They let down their net, those two,
While the morning sun dries up the grassy dew.

They rocked and rolled about,
hoping beyond hope that the shrimp were still out.

Suddenly calmness, no water roiling,
no more waves, nor rocking and rolling, no trawling.

It was as if the sea gods were scolding.
Their net went slack, the day's beauty was blackening.

Emotions gave way to hopelessness, then again found,
a way to gain blessings, they were bound.

Beyond Belief, their net was full,
and sunshine greeted them on their homeward pull.

What more could they ask of Him, on that high throne?
He had answered their silent prayers all on His own!

Angel of Fate

Tears flowing freely,
Sad and lonely,
Through and through,
You were taken from me,
And I, extremely blue.

Torn and desolate,
Contemplating suicide
With you no longer at my side,
And no one in whom to confide.

By myself, parking in the lot,
Looking up at a sharp knock.
A young, pretty Asian woman
Stood alone and in her hand a book.

My car window went down;
She handed it in,
As she said to me,
"God loves you, my friend."

Thinking to give it a toss,
Looking down, I saw a cross
Then up to thank her....
Seeing no one near!

Not a soul: Was she really there?

Page after page, read every night,
Words to live by give me great delight.
Words of Love, freely given in verse,

Evelyn Marie (Lott) Sanders

Words in which I became immersed.

Parking in that same lot,
I've never seen her again,
Wondering if that book came on a beam,
Hoping it was not just a dream.

Reflecting on that sweet innocent face,
Knowing she helped spare me
Through her own angelic grace,
From that suicidal fate.....

By: Evelyn Marie (Lott) Sanders after the Death of Michael Sanders

Not Me

He wanted you, not me....
I wanted you, but He won the bid...
My breath almost left, the moment yours did...
But, He took you, not me.

Thought things went in two by two...
No, He didn't want me; He wanted you...
Do I move on alone?
Can't, half of me is gone.

I lay my head and cry...
Cause, I just want to die...
There'll never be another...
Can't have one without the other.

Thought we would last longer...
Even so, today my love is stronger...
But left to roam this lonely sea...
Cause, He took you, not me.

Evelyn Marie (Lott) Sanders

Follow

Can you see me?
I'm over here.
We can finally be..
This is for me and you...
Can I carry your gear?
Don't hide behind those flowers of blue....
Are those eyes of fear?
Look, look I'm waving now.....
Can you see me?
That's a big red spot on your brow!
Foggy glasses, can't see......
Blood's dripping down my face.
What's going on here?
Falling, falling in this space.......
Hear me, see my tear.
Do you see??
Father, quick, I'm asking for Grace!
Please, I need Your Gra........

Crazy Pay Raises

Politicians need it,
Decreed by them,
But unvoted in.

Teachers seek it,
Admittedly for survival,
But noted as trivial.

Insurance salesmen take it,
Unneeded by us,
But touted as a must.

Bankers protect it,
Trusted by people,
But checked out in triple.

Lawyers have it,
Submitted in fees,
But charged to me.

Preachers collect it,
Tossed by us in plates,
But opened no gates.

We aren't paid it,
Created in those work mazes,
Those Crazy Pay Raises!

"Golden Poet Award" Winner of World of Poetry Magazine's contest, April, 1989, when teaching 7th and 8th grade reading at Springfield Middle

School. The presentation took place in Washington, D.C. on September 2nd at the fifth annual meeting of the Poetry Convention.

Crate Number 2

By Steve Patrick

-1-

At age ten, Harlan James Rugger read his first Hardy Boys Mystery novel, *The Haunted Fort*, and became addicted to reading and detective stories. From then onward, fictional investigators Sherlock Holmes, Hercule Poirot, Reggie Fortune, Inspector Maigret, and other sleuths, those famous and those obscure, became part of his life. As he read, the race was on to see if he could unravel a baffling array of clues and uncover the evildoer before the sleuth.

The bane of his school years was Charlotte Taylor, who at lunch hour would say as loud as a ship's foghorn, "He's the guy who reads about people who don't exist."

The literature teacher, Mr. Clements, overheard the jab and called Harlan aside. "Forget small people, and remember, a person without imagination is a person who will not – ever - enjoy life." The next day the educator turned over a list of titles and said, "You might enjoy these works by lesser-known mystery authors. I also enjoy a good whodunit."

With Mr. Clements as an ally, Harlan led an unconventional teenage life of keeping to himself to read. One unexpected bonus materialized. By maintaining a straight-A average, he graduated as the salutatorian. Then, in the fall, he was wished good luck by family and friends as he started four years of a fully paid scholarship at Kenneth Quincy Emmerson, a liberal arts college.

During the summer hiatus, he worked at his uncle's delivery service, thus allowing his pockets to have extra spending money not supplied by the scholarship. With the absence of his birth father, who was hopelessly trapped in corporate America, Uncle Jeff became a surrogate. The two would go fishing or walk along Elm Crest Street as Harlan kicked around his teenage experiences, days at school, and the latest whodunit. When he reached twelve, Uncle Jeff gave counsel on the changes in his body and taught him to accept and adjust to a new him as he passed through puberty and his voice dropped. One day, his uncle said, "You'll be needing these soon," and handed over a kit with a razor, shaving cream, after-shave.

Four years of college passed quickly. When commencement came, there was no post-graduation plan. Thus, Harlan stayed at *JKR Transport* as the dispatch bill-of-lading clerk for the summer but felt he was floating with no purpose in life. Had a life of reading detective stories not prepared him for the outside world?

On a Friday night, Uncle Jeff said, "I've watched you work these last few summers. You're efficient and accurate, but your heart isn't in commerce. You belong in academia. Have you thought of teaching?"

"I have," came the reply, "but nine to five in a schoolroom with repetitive courses year after year facing rows of students, most of whom don't care to learn, isn't for me."

Uncle Jeff nodded understanding. "I was restless my first year after finishing at State, and only became content when I started a business of my own, *JKR Transport*, and with the decision realized I held my destiny in my hands. Not surprisingly, because I enjoyed my chosen goal, the company became prosperous, and the time came to consider marriage. So, I wed your Aunt Rebecca. I suggest you consider owning your own business, and never forget that you're the only person you have to please. There! I'll say nothing more. See you Sunday at the BBQ."

Harlan turned over the night deliveries and pick-ups to Louise, the oncoming clerk. During the walk home, he began mulling over his uncle's idea to own a business, his business. Saturday was spent in a cocoon of thinking as he wandered aimlessly through the city. Then, on Sunday morning, a concept came, thoughts were arranged, and he called Mr. Clements, the literature teacher in high school.

Mr. Clements took pleasure in seeing ex-students, and he said, "Yes, of course, come over, and we'll brainstorm."

Later that morning, when Harlan left his high school mentor, a decision was set in stone. Now he was left with a knotty problem of breaking the news to his parents. Being an only child, he was expected to succeed in life. His father, who judged the world by material wealth, would say, "I'm waiting for the day you pull into the driveway at the wheel of a Mercedes."

Sunday afternoon, he dressed for the barbeque, took a breath, and went into the backyard where steaks and bratwurst awaited the grill. Throughout the meal, everyday family chatter filled any voids in eating. Harlan talked with his uncle's wife, Becky, who he hadn't seen since the last get-together. He wondered why the couple didn't have children but left the mystery a mystery.

As the party wound down, he picked his moment and stood to get everyone's attention.

To his father's dismay, he announced plans to start his own business using a skill in which he was an expert.

Uncle Jeff gave him a thumbs up.

-2-

Despite the doomsayers and naysayers from this family and friends, Harlan started *The Whodunit* bookstore on meager savings and a loan from his uncle. His mother, Aunt Becky, Uncle Jeff, Mr. Clements, and well-wishers attended the opening. Missing was his father lost, again, to the corporate world.

For the first weeks, the cynics proved to be prophets, and one night, after studying the dismal ledger sheet, he said aloud to rows of unsold books, "I can hold on for five months, then the rent's due."

On the morning of the beginning of the fourth week, a Siamese cat carrying a dead mouse by the scruff of the neck sat on its haunches in front of him. The gift was dropped at Harlan's feet. "Are you worried I'll miss my dinner?" A broom and dustpan were pulled from the closet, and Harlan asked, "And to whom do you belong?" The visitor hopped onto the desk and sat watching the cleanup. The contribution to the bookstore went into the trash to be removed before closing. Out of sensitivity to the customers, a section of the morning newspaper obscured Mickey's remains. To the seal point, Harlan said, "You look well cared for, and you don't have the physical wounds of an alley cat." The Siamese began a face washing ritual. "Very well, you may stay until closing, then back out with your buddies."

At nine, the visitor was nowhere to be found, and the assumption there had been an exodus was made.

When the bookshop opened at eleven the following morning, the Siamese was on the checkout desk, and watched as the door was unlocked, swung to the side, and hooked to the wall.

Facing the seal point, Harlan said, "You can't stay here. There's no doubt you have papers, and your owner must be frantic." The feline yawned. "Very well, but you'll have to leave some time to find food, and I'm sure Ma Nature will call." There was a pause. "You are housebroken?"

With clipboard in hand, Harlan began the morning routine of taking inventory to match against yesterday's receipts.

The first customer arrived and began to peruse titles. Presently, a credit card was swiped, and the man left with four books. Throughout the day, there was an ebb and flow of customers.

At closing, Harlan looked for the Siamese. Again, the search proved fruitless. He tallied the receipts and added them a second time to confirm his calculations. There was a profit not only for the day but for the week.

The following morning, fresh from a bank deposit, Harlan came into the shop from living quarters at the back to open the shop for the day. Again, a cursory search revealed no Siamese.

He turned at the sound of a voice.

"Good morning." Before him was a woman in her forties. "I've been everywhere," she babbled, her eyes searching his face. "You're my last hope. Do you have the mystery, *Out*?"

There was a faint hope in the voice when she asked, and Harlan thought the woman might collapse when he said, "By Natsuko Kirino? Yes."

He pulled the book from the shelf, quoted a price, and handed the novel to eager hands. The woman pulled the book to her breasts and gushed, "The perfect birthday gift. I would have paid twice - three times - the amount. You've saved my life." As a shaking hand surrendered a Discover Card, the Siamese hopped onto the windowsill.

After signing, the woman said, "I'll be back. I'll be back," and sailed out the entrance. Customers arrived, books came off shelves throughout the day, and by nine that evening, *The Whodunit* was firmly in the black.

The Siamese jumped onto the desktop, and man and animal faced the other for a long moment. Harlan capitulated. "Come on. I hope you'll like a warmed-over casserole." The two walked the passage to the rear-of-the-store living quarters, food was prepared for two, and silence while eating befell the kitchen. At length, with the dishes cleaned, both human and beast were asleep by eleven.

But Harlan's rest was fitful. He woke remembering Pyewacket in *Bell, Book, and Candle,* and using the ambient light in the bedroom, looked at the Siamese asleep on a chair cushion and made a snap-of-the-fingers decision. "You brought me the gift of a mouse. And so, I christen you, Mouser. Not an imaginative name but precise. There the issue is settled, and you're a member of the bookstore." He leaned back on the pillow, and as sleep took over, thought, *I'll have to buy cat food.*

He blinked.

Sunshine streamed through the window and began filling the room with morning light. He looked at the Siamese curled on the chair. "Okay, Mouser, let's see if yesterday's omen holds, and don't you dare leave the shop." He swung from the bed, walked into the bathroom, and emerging freshly groomed and dressed, was ready to face what the day brought.

The Siamese was not in the bedroom or the kitchen.

Harlan fixed scrambled eggs with pork sausage. No fawn-colored seal point came to eat. "Oh, well," he said, "you do have your own life as a vagabond, it seems." He entered the shop. Mouser sat on the windowsill and watched the ritual of opening for the day.

There were customers in the store throughout the afternoon, and *The Whodunit* produced more revenue in one day than the previous week. A delighted Harlan happily tallied the receipts, turned to Mouser, and said, "We can't afford a Mercedes – yet - but we're on our way."

-3-

Harlan read each new book before it reached the shelf. Thus, if a clientele asked specifics about the mystery, he explained the intricacies of the plotline without revealing the ending. Or, as he joked, *The Whodunit* doesn't divulge Whodunit. Within the month, the store was famous enough for people to drive fifty miles to browse, discuss, and buy the latest hard or softcover coming off the presses. He mingled and chatted with the customers and chanced to overhear a woman wish she could get a book for her child in this store and not have to go to *The Bo Peep Bouquet for Tykes* to buy a Dr. Seuss.

Harlan eyeballed a sparsely filled bookshelf against the wall and placed an order for a half dozen Dr. Seuss books. The dealer listed a variety of gardening publications on a split-screen, and because *The Whodunit* was a first-time customer, the bookstore could choose a landscaping pictorial. On impulse and not sure they would sell in a mystery shop, he bought three covers with the assurance FedEx would deliver within two days. "Now let's see if the woman buys or if it was smoke," he said to Mouser sitting on the credenza beside the desk. "But my feline friend, mysteries remain the store's heart."

The Whodunit's supremacy in the world of mystery was solidified when again Harlan paid attention to an overheard remark. The customer wanted a place to meet and discuss the latest finds in the world of crime in the evening and away from the clatter of coffee shops. On Friday, a signup list to gauge genuine interest was available at the checkout desk. On Sunday evening at the six o'clock closing, there were twenty-nine names, phone numbers, and email addresses. A second survey was conducted. By consensus of the twenty-nine names, the first and third Wednesdays of the month from seven-thirty to nine became the time to meet for a roundtable. After two meetings, Harlan realized a fact of literary life. Mystery readers are voracious readers.

The third meeting stretched to nine-thirty before the chattering members left. Harlan didn't mind. Several new novels left with the departing readers. He shut the door, turned the key, and after letting out a puff of air, leaned against the jamb.

Mouser, atop the checkout desk, began his preening ritual.

-4-

Harlan was grateful when the large Regulator Clock with Roman numerals signaled nine o'clock. The door was locked, and the CLOSED sign switch flipped up, allowing the window reflected a soft dark-orange glow.

"Time to tally the books," he said with a wink to Mouser. "I predict there'll be enough for two bags of Meow Mix today. Still, buying our Mercedes isn't possible. But someday, we'll arrive in the mater's and pater's driveway and watch jaws drop."

As he pulled the sales tray from the top drawer, the telephone rang.

"The bookstore is closed," he said aloud and glanced at the screen readout. The incoming call was from *JRK Transport.*

Harlan's eyes narrowed and, with a sense of anxiety, muttered, "At this time of night?"

Mr. Bell's invention persisted, and the receiver was lifted. "*Whodunit Bookstore.*"

"Good evening, my favorite and only nephew." As customary when speaking on the phone, Uncle Jeff's voice was pitched a decibel higher than normal conversation. "Charlotte Taylor will be at your store tomorrow morning."

"Ah, yes, Miss Congeniality of the high school lunchroom." Then, and not hiding the irritation in his voice, Harlan asked, "And to what do I owe this dubious pleasure? The woman cannot put two sentences together that make sense, looks and acts like the *Hulk's* sister, and sounds like a braying donkey when she laughs."

"And why the woman is good at landscaping. The flowers are threatened, and they obey."

"My appreciation of plant life has diminished, but she is coming here for what senseless reason."

"You're the only person I know who can field this one. Some old duffer died and left Charlotte a crate of books, and to say she's upset is an understatement."

"Because she received books?"

"And why I'm sending her to *The Whodunit.* You quote Chaucer."

"No one quotes Chaucer," Harlan said.

"My delivery man is on his way with the crate, and Gus, by name, is irked."

Harlan suppressed a laugh at hearing irked.

"The delivery caused over time, and tonight, Gustaf Alström will miss a beer or two with his gang at the booze hall."

"Why are you sending the crate at this time of night?"

"The crate of books didn't arrive on the delivery dock until after six, and Charlotte didn't get here until eight. I told her about your bookstore. And added, you're the one who can give answers as to their worth. I was told by MS Taylor, and I quote, 'Send them there tonight, and I'll be at his store at eight.'"

"Mouser and I don't open until eleven."

"Exactly why I am calling you and why the crate is in transit. Charlotte will be standing in *The Whodunit* tomorrow at eight with or without an open door."

Harlan resigned himself and said, "I'll wait for the books, and I'll open for Charlotte at eight."

"Atta boy! Let me know the outcome once the dust settles."

The receiver found the cradle, and Harlan said, "Plan an escape, Mouser. We're to be invaded by a wrecking crew of one. But, at least, you can hide under the desk."

A burly man with a dolly loomed outside the store window and, without waiting for permission, pushed against the closed door.

The sales tray found its place in the desk drawer, then making no effort to move with alacrity, Harland sauntered to the front and opened the barrier.

With shirt buttons strained, Gus showed the effect of time spent in the booze hall with friends. "Didn't Mr. Rugger call and say I was a-comin'."

Knowing the man would not grasp the sarcasm, Harlan said, "The door is bolted to avoid surly customers."

A hefty wooden crate - perched on the dolly - came through the doorway and was dropped in the center of the room. An electronic pad was presented, and Gus grunted, "Here. Need a signature."

The seal point began an inspection of the sides of the box as Harlan digitally signed the display screen.

"The office will send ya a bill." Gus, the irked deliveryman, pushed the dolly through the entrance and left.

After locking the door, Harlan shook his head and said, "He must be Charlotte's brother. Was there a Hulk II?

Mouser hopped atop the crate and began pawing at the die-stamped number 2.

The well-constructed wooden case was made of #1 Grade Yellow Pine. The corners were mitered and fastened with screws. *Expensive home for a stash of books,* Harlan thought. A ghoulish idea popped into his head. "Careful, Mouser. There may be a dead body squinched inside. But I ask you, my feline friend, shall we open the box? And I answer you and me by saying, why shouldn't we? After all, possession is nine-tenths of the law. The canon is written in a dust-covered law book somewhere."

He went to the back of the store, returned with a cordless power drill, and with screws removed, lifted the top of the crate. Within were rows of leather-bound books protected by heavy quilted padding and a water-proof plastic sheet. "These ain't no off-the-shelf Wal-Mart books."

He pulled the first volume, cautiously opened the cover, and after reading the Copyright date, said, "Impossible. After all these years, the paper is pristine white, the print looks fresh from the press, and Mouser, I doubt these books have been read."

He spent the following two hours carefully scrutinizing and cataloging each treasure.

With the books replaced and the lid secured, he shook his head slowly and said, "A fortune."

Author's note:

There are few authors as widely known as Agatha Christie, considered the founder of modern mystery novels. Recently a signed first edition of her book, The Mysterious Affair at Styles, sold for $40,000.00 at auction.

The Monarch's Wife

By Mary E. McCaffrey

It was dark when Pearl took the coffee can down to the little creek located behind their house. In the summers, her children loved to chase crawfish in the sparkling water of the shallow creek, but the recent storm had caused the creek to overflow its narrow banks.

"I'm sorry, baby boy," she whispered as she wound up her arm and hurled the can as far as she could throw it into the flooded creek. The coffee can hit a rock, causing it to turn around and around until the whirling action of the water carried it away.

Where will his little soul go? Pearl wondered. Will it go full circle and wind up in the fertile, alluvial soil of the Mississippi Delta? Will it flow into the Mississippi River, then emerge into the Illinois River, and eventually wind up in a town called Swansea? Or will it settle in an unknown place somewhere between earth and sky?

One thing Pearl knew for certain; she would never forget him.

She had wrapped the dead baby in a receiving blanket and put him in an empty coffee can she had found in the kitchen. The infant's shroud was not made of fine linen, nor was it scented with cedarwood; rather, it was an old receiving blanket all three of her youngest children had used, and the makeshift coffin smelled of freshly-roasted coffee.

Pearl knew she was not responsible for either the baby's birth or his death, and she would forever regret she could not honor his brief life with a proper burial, but she had no choice. She had to sacrifice the dead child for the living one.

"Sommabitch! Bastard!" she screamed.

The hate she felt for her husband far exceeded any love she had ever felt for him. She had run out of the house shoeless, and the pine needles and pine cones cut her bare feet. Limping over to a dead log near the creek, she slumped down on it. Seated there, she desperately tried to figure out a plan. Pearl didn't like any of her choices, but knew she had to do something to protect her children.

Pearl sat there until the dark morning sky turned a soft white. Clouds as white as a French meringue slowly swirled around in the newborn sky. The sky looked too clean for the dirty work Pearl planned to do when she returned home.

Having sat there for hours pondering the horrible situation she was in, she realized she needed to get home to check on the children.

* * * * *

As soon as she returned home, Pearl loaded three 00 buck shotgun shells into her grandfather's 12 gauge shotgun and set it upright in the corner of the kitchen. After filling two bags with clothes and setting them near the door, she made a fresh pot of coffee.

Looking up at the cuckoo clock, she waited for the coffee to drip. It was shortly after 3:00 a.m.

Pearl poured a cup of the freshly-brewed coffee, but the smell of it made her feel sick when she thought of the dead baby. She pushed the cup away, unable to drink it.

Her hands were usually busy with cooking, cleaning, washing clothes, ironing, taking care of the endless demands of the children, and tending to her butterfly garden. Even when she had a moment to sit, her hands were still busy mending clothes, wiping runny noses, listening to the children's complaints, and reading her Bible in the evenings after the children were asleep.

Now, her hands were idle as she waited for her husband to come home.

More time passed as Pearl waited for Lucien, and she continued to rock and to think about the events in her life that had gotten her into this predicament.

* * * * *

When Pearl was a teenager, she hadn't known the first time a person falls in love is just a practice session--not to be confused with the real thing--more like the sound of thunder before lightning strikes or a warning shot in the air if an animal threatens to attack but with the gun pointed at the heart and not the head.

When she first met the man she would later marry, the eighteen-year-old Pearl was sitting in the football bleachers at Tallahatchie High School watching her younger sister, Ruby, practice her liberty cheerleading stunt.

Ruby stood on one leg flamingo-like on top of the pyramid, the other leg bent at a right angle, and her arms flung out in victory. She turned her head sideways, smiled as though posing for a picture, and dismounted by landing in the arms of two other cheerleaders.

Pearl's eyes wandered over to the other side of the football field where the boys, dressed in their gold and black uniforms, were running laps in the late September afternoon.

The new boy, over whom all the girls were gaga, sprinted past her several times, but never looked in her direction. He'd been at the school only a few months and had already dated a half dozen of the prettiest girls.

Pearl was not interested in him, but his courtship strategy fascinated her. His behavior reminded her of the beautiful butterflies in her daddy's butterfly magazines as he flitted from girl to girl like a Monarch butterfly sipping nectar from the cup-shaped flowers. Whether or not he was successful in his endeavors didn't alter his courtship strategy because, within a short time, he moved on to the next girl.

When football practice ended, the girls swarmed around him like hummingbirds searching for sugar water.

* * * * *

Most days when Pearl got out of class, she met Ruby at the football stadium and they walked home together. Today, however, when Pearl went to the stadium, Ruby's friend, Mark, told her Ruby had gone to get a Coke with two girlfriends.

The boys were playing cockroach poker, and the new boy was winning. He looked up from the cards he was holding, and a spark of interest shone in his eyes when he saw Pearl.

"Want to play some cards?" he asked.

"No, thank you," Pearl responded.

"Your name's Pearl, isn't it? Aren't you Ruby's sister?"

"Right on both counts," Pearl replied and started walking away because she wasn't interested either in playing cards or in him.

He hesitated a second, then asked, "Want to go get a Coke?"

Surprised he'd asked her out, but thinking he'd made a bet with one of the other boys that she would go out with him, Pearl's answer came easily, "No, thanks."

* * * * *

Over the next few weeks, Lucien persisted in asking her out.

Thinking he would lose interest in her as he had done with other girls once he dated them, Pearl agreed to go on a date with him. Pearl knew she wasn't his type. *Ruby, with her torch red hair and her joy de vivre, is more his type of girl,* Pearl thought, *not a white cabbage butterfly like me.*

Dating Lucien was like playing a game of cockroach poker, like trying to see which one would fake out the other. Pearl admitted he was a good kisser, but he'd had a lot more kissing experience than she'd had. After months of dating, the kissing sessions became intense.

Lucien said, "Damn it, Pearl, either put out or shut up," then smiled as if to soften his harsh words.

"I can't, Lucien, I promised Daddy I wouldn't until I got married."

"Then let's get married," Lucien demanded.

Pearl was frozen with indecision.

Thinking he was bluffing, she called him on it. "Okay."

* * * * *

Lucien and Pearl got married in Woodville, Mississippi, and, after checking into a Comfort Inn, Lucien went to get them something to eat.

Several hours later, fortified with a few drinks, Lucien returned to the motel room, threw a bag of hamburgers on the bed, silently stripped off his clothes, and got into bed butt naked.

Pearl timidly slipped on her gown and hurriedly got into bed beside her silent husband. Gone was the trail of butterfly kisses along her neck, and gone was the sweet talk that accompanied their former necking sessions. Fifteen minutes later, the marriage had been consummated.

Lucien turned onto his side and was soon snoring, and Pearl turned her face away as tears wet her pillow.

When Pearl and Lucien returned from their honeymoon, they moved into the old house where Lucien and his grandmother, Rose, had lived before her death some five years earlier. There was little furniture in the house because either it had fallen into disrepair and been discarded or it had been given away. The house was large enough for them and any future family they might have, and there was no rent to pay.

Pearl busied herself with cleaning the dust-filled house, and Lucien put up wooden shelves in the kitchen to hold the few pots and pans and the groceries they had.

After the house was in order, Pearl worked in the front yard, overgrown with milkweed plants, trumpet vines, some scraggly rose bushes, and lots of brambles. Milkweed plants growing on both inside and outside the fenced yard attracted butterflies. Like her daddy, Pearl loved butterflies, and planted other flowers that attracted them.

Soon the Monarch caterpillars crawled across the milkweed plants, voraciously devouring everything in their path until the few remaining leaves resembled fine French lace.

* * * * *

Lucien was rarely at home, either spending his days dogfighting or training his dogs to fight. Most nights, he was out drinking or catting around.

After one of Lucien's alcohol-fueled nights of carousing, Pearl asked him, "Why did you marry me, Lucien?"

His response was, "Because I knew you would never leave me." Then he added, "I also wanted to show your daddy he couldn't dictate who I should date."

Pearl said, "You mean because you wanted to date *me*?"

"No, Pearl, I wanted to date Ruby. When your daddy said 'no' his daughter couldn't date me, I decided I would show him."

"Lucien, my father didn't stop Ruby from dating you. She decided that for herself because you had a bad reputation."

"Well, I showed him, didn't I? If I couldn't date Ruby, I'd date you. You were my second choice, not my first."

On another night, Lucien asked Pearl a similar question as to why she had married him.

Aloud, she said, "Because I thought I loved you"; silently, she thought, *Looks like we both got a bad bargain.*

Neither one was happy in the marriage; but, when Pearl learned she was expecting a child, she realized she had another life to consider.

* * * * *

Three months later, Pearl was busy in her butterfly garden when she looked up to see her daddy's smiling face. She began to cry.

Wrapping his arms around his daughter, her daddy said, "It seemed like you dropped off the face of the earth, Pearl. I've been looking for you for a while. Finally, someone told me you and Lucien had moved into his grandmother's old house."

Pearl still had her arms wrapped around her daddy's neck.

"Are you disappointed in me for getting married, Daddy?"

"No, honey. You're old enough to make your own decisions."

She replied sadly, "Lucien said he told you we got married, and he said you didn't *want* to see me anymore."

"No, that isn't true. You are my daughter. I always want to see you. When he called, he said you were expecting a baby.

"No, Daddy, I kept my promise to you, but I am expecting a baby now. It's due in January."

* * * * *

From the time of Genevieve's birth, Lucien wanted nothing to do with the baby. She looked just like him but was flawed, and that embarrassed him. He suggested they place her in a home where she would get good care. Pearl looked into her baby's China doll blue eyes and balked at Lucien's suggestion. She even threatened to take the baby and leave him.

From then on, he showed no interest in Genevieve whatsoever. He never fed her, never changed her diaper, never played with her, and only picked her up when she was crying, and then only because Pearl asked him.

The doctor had told them the baby would never be like other children and had suggested they take her home and just love her.

* * * * *

When Genevieve was a year old, she had just begun to crawl.

At two years old, she was still not walking when Lucien Armand Bernard, Jr., was born. Lucien was proud of his son, whose only flaw Lucien perceived was his son's red hair.

When Junior was eleven-months-old, he began to pull up and to talk. The first time he said "Dada," Lucien whirled him around the room, then took his son on his lap in the armchair while the two continued their one-word conversation of "Dada."

With a sudden burst of energy, Genevieve, dressed in a diaper and a pink seersucker romper, crawled over to the armchair, pulled herself up by clutching onto Lucien's pants leg, and—to Pearl's amazement—parroted her younger sibling's "Dada."

Lucien didn't even look at his daughter but picked Junior up and walked away.

When Junior had begun talking, he couldn't say Genevieve's name, so he called her Nevie. Even though Junior mostly ignored Nevie, she loved him. Her simple explanation was, "He's my brother."

When the twins were born, she loved both of them. It was like she got two birthday presents. The three sisters played together and squabbled like most siblings. Now, at age eleven, Nevie had the same mental maturity as the five-year-old twins, Lula and Essie.

When Baby Pearl was born, Nevie was now twelve but still had not progressed beyond the mental age of five.

* * * * *

Pearl was busy planting Mexican sunflowers, and Nevie ran around the water fountain. Around and around the fountain she ran chasing a large Monarch butterfly until anyone watching couldn't have told who was chasing who. The wind blew Nevie's thin sundress against her tanned legs while the Monarch zigzagged in front of her.

Tired of playing tag, the Monarch hid among the other butterflies sunning themselves on the stones in the garden.

Instead of drinking the clean water from the water fountain, the butterflies preferred wallowing in the mud puddles.

A male Monarch butterfly, with eye-like dots on his hind wings, and a smaller, female Monarch butterfly sat side by side at the edge of the largest mud puddle and, with their straw-like mouths, sipped from the mud puddle like two sweethearts sharing a chocolate soda at the local five-and-dime.

* * * * *

Essie ran into the house slamming the screen door behind her with Junior following close behind.

"Mama, Junior said another bad word."

"What did he say?" Pearl asked her daughter.

Essie leaned against her mother and whispered, "He said 'butterflies fart,'" and her eyes got big and round with righteous indignation.

"It ain't a bad word," Junior defended. "In science class, Mr. Byrd talked about butterflies and he said the word 'fart.'"

"Did he use that exact word, Junior?"

"No, Ma'am, he said the word 'flatuous' and I asked him what it meant, and he said 'fart.'"

"Junior, don't say words that aren't polite to your sisters."

"Can I still show Essie how a goldfish belches, Maw?"

"That's enough schooling for today, mister. Your daddy should be home soon. Y'all go on and wash y'alls hands because the red beans are ready and all I need to do is cook the rice."

* * * * *

Pearl missed cooking red beans with Ruby. Her beautiful sister was now dead, having died in an automobile accident while coming home from the Piggly Wiggly.

Ruby had been the stronger spouse in the marriage and after her death, her husband Edd began drinking again and said he couldn't go back into their house because he kept seeing Ruby's presence everywhere. Edd asked Pearl if he could leave the two children, Cece and Jesse, with her while he went up North to find work.

Pearl's response was, "What's two more children in this house?"

* * * * *

When Lucien first saw Cece, he kept staring at her and exclaimed, "You are the spitting image of your mother. You don't recognize your Uncle Lucien, Cece? Want to come and give me a hug?"

Cece leaned against Pearl and whispered, "I don't like him," and Pearl thought, *I don't like him either,* and instantly felt guilty.

* * * * *

Cece stood beside Pearl's chair and watched as her aunt ripped out the old hem on one of Essie's dresses. She clutched her doll to her flat chest--a doll with only a few wisps of blonde hair and a bare, pink bottom--and watched as her aunt deftly whipped in the new hem.

Pearl looked up and asked, "What happened to Dolly, Cece?"

"Lulabug and them was playing beauty parlor and Nevie brushed all of her hair out, and Junior cut up all of her clothes. Dolly's not pretty anymore, but I still love her anyway."

"I know you do, Cece. "You know," Pearl added, "Nevie didn't do it on purpose. Will you be patient with her?"

"I'll try, Aunt Pearl, but it ain't easy. Junior says she's 'two slices short of a bread loaf' and tapped his head."

"I'll talk to Junior about not cutting up Dolly's clothes. It'll be okay," Pearl said, pulling her niece onto her ample lap.

Smiling, Pearl said, "Cece, you've outgrown that dress. I can see all the way to Christmas! We need to find you some more clothes, sweetie."

"But I want to keep this dress, Aunt Pearl. This is a store-bought dress Mama got me when I started first grade."

"I got some flour sacks with ballerinas on them, and I got some with rolling pins, teapots, kettles, and flour canisters on them too," Pearl teased. "Which ones would you like?"

"I like ballerinas, Aunt Pearl."

Then looking up at her aunt, Cece asked in a pensive voice, "Do you miss my mama, Aunt Pearl?"

Pearl looked at her niece who was the image of her sister at the same age, a tiny girl with wild, red hair like Orphan Annie on a bad hair day. She smiled again when she remembered a teenaged Ruby declaring Halo shampoo had been the only thing that tamed it.

"Yes, Cece, I miss her with all of my heart, but I will see her again in Heaven."

"But you never talk to Jesse and me about her, Aunt Pearl."

"I thought it would make you sad for me to talk about her."

"No, Jesse and me want to talk about her 'cause we miss her."

"Cece, when your mama and I was kids, we was always full of mischief. One time when I was in second grade and your mama was in the first grade, I stole a piece of licorice gum from a girl in my class and hid it in Ruby's drawstring bag where she kept her crayons. The teacher searched all the kids' bags, but I kept switching the hiding place and the teacher never found the gum. I tell you, Cece, I was a little devil, but I learned never to steal again because that gum tasted God-awful," Pearl said, chuckling at the memory.

Her rough hand rubbed Cece's back as she related more childish pranks she and Ruby were involved in, and the sound of the creaking rocker was the last sound Cece heard as she fell asleep.

* * * * *

The next day when the children were outside playing, Pearl stood in the hot kitchen ironing one of her husband's shirts, sweat dripping off her face.

Baby Pearl was in her highchair and every time she dropped her rattle, she cried. One of the twins would run inside, pick it up, and give it back to her. The drop-and-fetch-it game continued until Pearl demanded, "That's enough. There's enough flies in this house already and y'alls inviting more."

As she continued ironing, Lucien's grandmother's old, wrought-iron fan groaned and spit out a little cool air. The window air conditioner was broken, but Lucien continued to ignore it. Pearl looked at the Van Heusen label on the shirt and muttered, "The kids and I wear clothes made from flour sacks but he only wears store-bought clothes." She slapped the iron onto the shirt and it hissed back.

The screen door was shut to keep out the flies, but Pearl could hear her kids playing in the backyard. The girls were choosing husbands as though playing Red Rover.

"Jesse's going to be my husband," Lulabug declared. Jesse meekly walked over to her side of a "house" drawn in the dirt.

The other twin, five-year-old Essie, reluctantly chose Junior but warned, "If you start acting ugly, mister, Imma gonna divorce you."

Junior wanted desperately to be claimed by *somebody* so he sullenly kept silent.

Not wanting to be left out of the game, Nevie declared, "I've got a husband already."

"No, you don't, Nevie; you ain't old enough to be married," Essie stated.

"Yes, I do too."

"What's his name?"

I can't tell. It's a secret," Nevie explained. "Can I tell half a secret?"

"No, a secret is a secret, but you still ain't married."

Essie peered through the screen door at Pearl and said, "Mama, Nevie said she has a husband and I told her she don't but she said she does."

"Well, she don't," Pearl stated emphatically.

Then a little curious, she set the iron down. "Who did she say she married?"

"She didn't say. She said it was a secret."

"Well, go back and tell her, 'Mama said none of y'alls getting married until y'alls eighteen without my consent, and I ain't consenting to her getting married,' and make sure she understands me."

"Okay, Mama, but she ain't gonna be a bit happy about it 'cause she's gonna have to get a divorce," and Essie slowly walked back into the yard to deliver the bad news.

* * * * *

"Let's play the bug game," Essie's "new husband" said. "Essie, you go first, Junior politely suggested.

The children formed a circle and in a sing-song voice each child took turns chanting a word, "Litterbug . . . jitterbug . . . doodlebug . . . mudbug . . . ."

When it came Nevie's turn, she remained silent.

The next child took up the chant, "Lovebug . . . bedbug . . . ."

When it came Nevie's turn again, all heads turned toward her, but no one expected her to respond.

"Lulabug!" shouted Nevie and giggled.

"That's not a real word, retard," Junior declared.

When Pearl heard Junior call Nevie *that* word, she walked out onto the porch and motioned for him. "If I ever hear you say that word to your sister again, you will be standing in a corner with a blistered butt until you are twenty-one, understand me, mister?"

"Yes, ma'am."

"Now, tell your sister you're sorry."

"Sorry."

"No, say it like you mean it, Junior."

"I'm sorry I called you a bad name, Nevie. I won't do it again, okay?"

"That's okay, Junior. You're still my brother."

* * * * *

Having two more children in the household was a big adjustment for her children because there were more squabbles.

"Sissy, Junior stole my dollar bill and he pinched me with some pinchers," Jesse said and stuck out his skinny, unblemished arm for her to examine. Seeing the doubt on his sister's face, Jesse began to cry.

Cece knew something had happened. She walked around the yard, then picked up a tree limb left by a recent storm and, just like her arm had a mind of its own, whopped Junior on his head.

Junior let out a howl and seconds later Pearl came barreling through the front door, the screen door flapping behind her.

"What's all this rigmarole about?" Pearl demanded.

"Cece hit me on my head and I didn't do nothing, Maw," Junior said.

With one hand held behind her back with fingers crossed and, as if receiving holy inspiration, Cece pointed an accusing finger at Junior and stated, "Junior stole Jesse's dollar bill, Aunt Pearl. The one Daddy gave him."

"Didn't," Junior denied.

"Did," Cece stated more firmly and Jesse silently nodded his head in agreement.

"I didn't steal his dollar bill," Junior stated emphatically. "I just borrowed it. I was being his banker."

"How are you going to be his banker?" Pearl demanded.

"I was going to give Daddy the dollar to bet on the dog fight and when Jesse's money doubled, then he'd have a dollar and so would I."

Well, you can kiss your money goodbye, mister, because there ain't gonna be any dog fighting in this house."

Annoyed, Pearl demanded, "Junior, empty your pockets."

Junior resisted, "Aw-w, Maw."

Seeing the look on his mother's face, he emptied one pocket and pulled out a silver-wrapped slice of Juicy Fruit gum stuck to a folded dollar bill. "It's mine but I'll give it to you, Jesse," Junior said grudgingly.

Cece excitedly pointed at the innocent bill and said, "That's Jesse's dollar bill, Aunt Pearl. He always folds it that way. Junior's not going to steal *my* dollar 'cause I'm saving it for some Halo shampoo," she stated defiantly.

Seeing the guilt on her son's face, Pearl demanded, "Now, mister, empty the other pocket and if you don't do it right now, I've a mind to jerk a knot in your tail."

"But, Maw—"

* * * * *

Pearl returned from the Goodwill store loaded with sacks filled with used clothes.

The six children sat on the front porch strangely silent with heads hung down.

"Who died?" Pearl asked jokingly.

Nevie started wailing and said, "Snowball, Mama."

At first, the words didn't register in Pearl's mind.

Snowball was not a "people cat," but she loved Pearl and Nevie. She'd wrap her tail around Pearl's leg when she wanted to be picked up or when she was hungry. When Pearl was busy, Nevie played with Snowball, brushed her fur, and the kitten often followed her around to Nevie's delight.

Now, none of the other children said anything, so Pearl demanded, "What happened?"

"We killed Snowball, Mama," Lula confessed.

Pearl demanded, "Who killed Snowball?"

No one said anything but five small fingers pointed at Junior.

He kept his head down, his arms wrapped around his head.

"We were just playing, Maw. We just wanted to see Brutus and Snowball play together."

Gall rose up in Pearl's throat and she said, "Junior stop lying! Dogs and cats don't play together. They don't talk the same language. They are just born that way.

"Tell me what happened!" Pearl demanded.

"Junior was practicing his dog fighting," Essie intervened. "When Snowball scratched Brutus on the nose, Brutus got angry and bit her. Then Snowball scratched him again, and then Brutus got really mad and bit her again. We didn't know Brutus would kill Snowball, Mama."

"Junior tried to pull them apart but Brutus was too strong, so we all ran away," Essie added.

Shocked at hearing about her pet's death, Pearl screamed, stuffed her fist in her mouth in an attempt to control herself, and ran toward the woods.

A little later, Junior walked slowly up to his mother. The freckles stood out more prominently on his pale face. "Maw? Mama, I'm sorry. I didn't know Brutus would kill Snowball. I'm really sorry, Mama. I promise, I will never dog fight again."

Brutus had dragged the kitten's bloody corpse into the woods. Patches of bloody, white fur blown from the yard now clung to a nearby mulberry tree.

When Pearl saw the body of her kitten, she pushed the dry leaves aside and frantically dug into the soft soil until there was a grave for it. She then demanded Junior bury the kitten he was responsible for killing. Pearl covered the grave with more dry leaves and placed two sticks in the form of a cross on it.

* * * * *

The next day Nevie held up a Mason jar in front of Pearl's face. The jar held two fireflies winking and blinking at Pearl.

"Flies, Mama. They's my pets. I don't want a dog. They's too loud," she explained.

"Well, you sure got your wish because there ain't gonna be a squeak outta these two," Pearl confirmed.

Suspicious as to where Nevie got one of her prized Mason jars, Pearl asked, "Where did you get one of Mama's canning jars?"

"Junior borrowed it so he could build a house for my pets, Mama. He put holes in the top so theys can breathe and he put paper towels on the floor so theys can wipe they's dirty feet," Nevie said proudly and held the Mason jar up closer to Pearl's face.

"Junior? *My* Junior?"

Nevie nodded her head.

"Wonders never cease," Pearl exclaimed and made no further mention of the purloined canning jar.

* * * * *

Lucien walked into the kitchen and slapped a twenty-five-pound sack of flour on the kitchen table and a white cloud rose from the sack.

"Pearlie Mae, we are walkin' in high cotton now, ain't we?" Rubbing his wife on her butt, Lucien leaned down to nuzzle her neck, suggestively rolling his eyes, and said, "How about we party tonight?"

"I ain't got time for no foolishness tonight, Lucien. Genevieve is sick. She's had a bellyache off and on all evening. I gave her some apple cider vinegar with honey, but I am not going to leave her alone until she is feeling better. There ain't gonna be no baby-making activities in this house tonight."

When Pearl turned to see her son standing in the doorway holding a smaller sack of sugar over his shoulder, she stopped talking and returned to stacking cans of food on the half-full shelves as Lucien quietly left to go to his truck.

Slapping the bag of sugar on the table as he'd seen his father do with the bag of flour, Junior proudly proclaimed, "I'm going to be as strong as my daddy pretty soon." He then followed his daddy out the door.

A few minutes later, Junior returned carrying more commodities. "Maw, Daddy left the rest of the groceries on the front porch and he told me to tell ya he's gone to see a man about a dog."

Pearl just rolled her eyes.

When Junior went to tell his sisters supper was ready, he said, "I heard Maw and Daddy arguing and she told him there ain't gonna be no more babies in this house and, if there was" (he then whispered), "she'd cut off his wiener." He continued his story. "Then Maw told him if he didn't like it, her and her kids would get along just fine, and he could hit the road, Jack."

* * * * *

A little later when Pearl walked into Nevie's bedroom, she saw her daughter had been crying and asked, "Are you pitching a hissy fit?" She smiled at the idea of her sweet-natured child doing that and followed up with, "Or did you eat too much candy today, sweetie?"

"No, Mama, no candy. I tee-teed in my bed. I sorry, Mama," and her blue eyes got bluer as though she was going to cry again.

"It's okay, sweetie. I'll change the sheets."

Pearl pulled back the sheets. They were not only wet but bloody. A tiny baby lay between Nevie's legs. The infant, a boy, was no larger than a sweet potato, its skin as transparent as gossamer silk, and had the tiniest fingernails. Pearl touched the infant's arm to see if he was alive, and the infant's toothpick arm recoiled as though Pearl's touch burned.

The baby gave a tired sigh and stopped breathing.

His face was familiar to Pearl. She had seen the same face on all five of her children when they were born.

Pearl's head hurt, then the pain travelled past her heart, and settled in a knot in her stomach.

"Doll?" Nevie asked, reaching out to pick up the dead baby.

"No—" Pearl said, then quickly changed her answer, "Yes, 'doll.' I'll put the doll in her bed."

Pearl wrapped the afterbirth in the soiled sheets and gave Nevie half a pain pill that had been left over from when she had Baby Pearl six months previously.

When she saw Nevie was about to fall asleep, Pearl said, "You go to sleep now, sweet girl."

"Okay, Mama," Nevie said with a sigh as her eyelids fluttered shut.

* * * * *

Excited little yelps and the rattle of the heavy chain around Lucifer's neck were familiar sounds as the puppies and Lucifer recognized the sound of Lucien's truck approaching the house.

Lucifer howled when he saw Lucien.

"Shut up, Lucifer! I'm your boss, and you're gonna learn that even if it kills you."

Then a click of the door and Lucien walked in.

When he saw Pearl sitting in the rocker with the coffee cup on the table and the shotgun lying across her lap, he hesitated for a moment before saying, "Mind if I have a cup of coffee, Pearl?"

"If you don't mind it cutting into your three minutes, Lucien," his wife responded.

"Three minutes?"

"You have three minutes to choose," Pearl said, lifting the shotgun from her lap.

"One, you can leave this house tonight and I suggest you never come back to Miss'sippi again."

Raising the shotgun chest high, she continued, "Two, I'll contact Sheriff Kemp and tell him what you done to our daughter. Since he has daughters of his own, I don't think he'll take kindly to it."

Lowering the shotgun eleven inches down from the center of his belt buckle, Pearl steadied the shotgun in her hands. "Three, I can shoot you right now." Coolly and calmly she added, "That's really my *first* choice, Lucien."

"Now, Pearlie," he said condescendingly and sniggered, "you don't know how to shoot a gun."

Pearl looked him in the eyes and asked, "Didn't you ever wonder why most Miss'sippi women carry a gun in their trucks, Lucien? For your information, my daddy taught all four of us girls how to shoot. Even if I don't kill you, I'm close enough to shoot you where it will hurt the most. One thing for sure, you will never be able to hurt another child. If you don't believe me, try me."

Lucien looked into his wife's eyes, shifted his eyes to the shotgun held steadily in her hands, and weighed his choices.

Leaning over to pick up the bags, he said, "I gotta get my gun before I leave, Pearl."

"It's in the bottom of the bag, Lucien."

Warily, he picked up the two bags filled with his belongings and walked toward the door. It clicked behind him.

A few minutes later, an angry howl came from Lucifer as he recognized his enemy. A shot rang out, the dog whimpered, and then was silent.

* * * * *

Nevie was still asleep when the other children woke up.

Pearl placed a pan of angel biscuits and a jar of mayhaw jelly in the center of the kitchen table.

"Please, please, Mama, can we have some hot chocolate and can I say the 'Thank you, Jesus' this time?" Lula begged.

Baby Pearl was in her highchair, a sprig of red hair falling like a baby whale's water spout on top of her head.

Pearl attempted to feed the baby rice cereal, but Baby Pearl continued to grab at the spoon wanting to feed herself. Realizing she was not going to win this battle, Pearl handed the baby the spoon. More cereal was in Baby Pearl's hair, on the table, and on the floor than got into her mouth.

There were no barking dogs, the children were squabbling as usual and, when Baby Pearl burped, they laughed.

Tomorrow, Pearl promised herself, she would tell her children their father had left. Tomorrow, Pearl vowed, she and her children would have a come-to-Jesus meeting at which she would explain in the simplest terms possible the changes she planned to make regarding their family and why they needed to make the changes.

But today would be a day of grace, a day of sharing jelly-filled biscuits and hot chocolate with her children.

The End

Wishes Can Come True

By Kathryn J. Martin

Looking out the Southern Pacific train window at the Arizona countryside, at nine years old, I made a wish.

Within minutes, my wish almost came true and scared me half to death...

* * * * *

My father, a retired Illinois Central Railroad derrick engineer, wanting to do something special for Mother and me, had arranged train passes for the trip of a lifetime.

Starting from nearby New Orleans, we would travel to Southern California, on up the West Coast to Seattle, across the northwestern states to Chicago and back down the I.C. mainline to our Ponchatoula in Southeast Louisiana.

Once the trip started, my older parents were content to stay in their coach seats and enjoy the view.

Naturally, at my young age, I could sit still only so long. When I grew restless--or to keep me from running her crazy--Mama would suggest I go stand for a while.

So, I'd take my place out of people's way in the wider corridor area across from the water fountain with its white cone-shaped paper cups.

Safety bars bolted to the window casing gave me something to hold onto in the swaying car and a place to rest my chin as I stood gazing longingly at the sights.

I was entranced by the scenery so much like the few Westerns I'd seen with their golden sandy deserts, big boulders and rushing streams.

How different it was from our part of Louisiana with its bayous, canals and swamps, not to mention our tall pines and huge live oaks draped with Spanish moss. Everything all subtropical - thick, green and lush.

103

Looking out at this new terrain, I felt I could see forever, as sometimes it took hours to near a mountain we'd been watching since daylight.

Long before we reached Arizona I was hooked for life on travel and its beauty.

And, secretly, I just *knew* I'd see my heroes from radio—Gene Autry and Roy Rogers!

In one place, on a bluff as high as the train roof but far enough away to allow me to look up and directly over at him – a cowboy complete with white Western hat, red shirt and tan leather chaps came riding up full blast.

He reined in so quickly to stop near the edge of the rim that his palomino almost sat on its haunches making dust fly!

It wasn't Gene or Roy but it didn't matter—I was finally seeing a *real cowboy in real life*!

Even in that few seconds the scene indelibly imprinted itself in my mind and I can see it 'til this day.

Talk about exciting!

Put that experience together with all the beautiful wide-open country where I probably could ride a *real* horse on a *real* ranch – well, I knew what I wanted.

I wanted to get off and run in the sand and dust, touch the rocks, wade in the clear streams rushing over boulders...

But I was inside a fast-moving train and no way could I get off.

That's when I made a wish followed by a promise to myself: I wish I could get off now but when I get big, I'm gonna get me a car and come back out here so I can stop and see things up close!

Well, it was a lot sooner than planned I almost got the first part of my wish...

For in a few minutes, the train slowed and teachers came from the car ahead leading a long line of quiet little Native American children, all headed for the last car behind us and their prearranged special stop to end their field trip.

The young boys and girls and I stared at each other from our dark eyes, wide with surprise at how much we looked alike--especially we girls with our black glossy hair in pigtails and our plain cotton print dresses. With my

French and Spanish Louisiana heritage and my unknown tribe of Native American Kentucky heritage, I was even the same color!

I continued to watch them as they watched back at me as they disappeared into the next car and the door closed behind them.

I guess we looked more alike than I'd thought, for as the train was grinding to a stop to let them off in the desert, I suddenly felt firm hands on my shoulders, dislodging me from my hold on the window bars.

I thought it was Mama or Daddy until I heard the voice of a stranger--kind, but still a stranger and I'd been warned about *them*!

"Good thing I found you," the railroad hostess said at the same time I felt her grip, "or you'd have gone on to California and I *know* you want to be with the rest of your little friends."

I was so startled, all I could do was work my mouth and stutter, "Uh, I, uh, I, uh," as she pushed me on past the restrooms toward the exit door beyond.

I was going to get my wish to stay in this beautiful country, run in the dust and sand, wade in the cool creek water, maybe ride a horse and visit a ranch...

But all of a sudden - I wanted only Mama and Daddy!

Behind me, several rows away and just in time, Mama turned to check on me.

Breaking into laughter, she called out, "She's *ours*! She's with *us*!"

(I guess she really loved me, for sometimes I got on her nerves so badly-it's a wonder she didn't stay silent and let me get off!)

Would you believe only a few days later we were visiting a museum in Oregon when I again felt the hands of a stranger on my shoulders - except this time I was standing with my parents and my uncle we were visiting.

And this time, you'd better believe, I wasn't making any wishes at all!

But the soft voice brought a message similar to the one on the train: "I know you'd be a lot happier with your little friends across the room."

Sure enough, as I was turned about by another pair of firm hands, I looked over to see another class field trip of Native American children from whom the museum curator thought I'd become separated.

This time, before the lady pushed me farther in what she assumed was the right direction, Uncle, Daddy and Mama all three spoke up to my rescue!

I managed to make the rest of that nineteen-day trip without being separated from my folks and soon matured enough to realize I wouldn't be.

It was then I remembered without fear my wish to travel and re-visit places we saw from the train windows.

Starting in sixth grade, I began to collect road maps and plan those trips—trips we couldn't take because we didn't have or even need a car!

But when I was thirteen, we did get one and nearly every Sunday afternoon, I sat in the car and took trips vicariously to all my favorite places.

Little did I know that years later I'd become an author and inspirational speaker and travel all across the United States and Canada, at first driving everywhere on speaking tours.

All those Sunday afternoons of imaginary travel paid off—I have never once gotten lost or disoriented.

In fact, twice in all the thousands of miles before GPS, my built-in north-east-south-west feelings didn't match the maps and both times there was a mistake in them and I was correct!

Even during the years since, I've had to give highway directions to hosts in their own home territories after being met at airports and heading to lodging and speaking areas!

Yes, it took a long time to have my wish to travel come true but now I not only get to walk the trails, wade the streams, climb the hills and boulders—I have the added bonus of meeting the friendly people in all those places.

What a treat to eat their foods, learn their customs, see in real what my history books told!

Wishes really *do* come true—in their own time and in their own way.

Make a wish or two and see!

The End

Belly Flops

By Mary Beth Magee

Everyone else was grieving. The room quivered with the sorrow gathered there. They stared at the broken body under the thin sheet and released fresh waves of grief, a veritable tsunami of sadness. The symphony of sobs drew on the sighs, beeps, and whistles of equipment for accompaniment.

If anyone of them had noticed me in the corner, they might have wondered why I didn't join my tears to theirs. Would they think me hard or calloused, unfeeling? Perhaps they would assume I didn't care about the young man swathed in bandages and sprouting tubes in every direction? Maybe they would account my lack of tears to shock.

None of them could guess the truth. I could hear him. His body may have been nearly destroyed, but his mind was alert and active.

"Can you get them to please shut up?" he asked again inside my head. "Two days of this caterwauling is enough. I'm trying to concentrate on dying here."

"I don't think they will listen," I thought back. "They figure you're done for, dying bit by bit and they want everyone to know how they feel. Any minute now, I expect them to request another box of tissues to dry their tears. Your parents are the worst of the lot."

"I'm not surprised. They wouldn't listen to me before, so why would they hear me now?"

"So why can *I* hear you? Haven't you wondered about that?"

"Makes sense to me, Jocelyn. You heard me long before the wreck. You listened to what I said, what I felt. We had a lot of great conversations. We're just continuing old habits, in a slightly different fashion."

"Good theory," I replied. "Not sure I believe it, but what the hay?"

"Connections, babe, that's what it's all about. Our connection is still intact."

He had a point there. I could feel the psychic wire stretching between our minds. It vibrated with the energy of his thoughts.

"So, Jocelyn, I'm gonna cut out of here soon. I want you to do a favor for me, please."

"If I can. What do you need?"

"You tell my folks to remember I signed my license to be an organ donor. Remind them I want some good to come out of this. And tell them I'm fine, I'm just going ahead. We'll meet up again later. Tell them 'no more belly flops,' okay?"

"Will they hear me anymore than they heard you?"

"Dunno, but I want you to try. It's getting harder to reach you and I don't know how much more I can send to you. But thank you for being my friend all these years. Thank you for hearing me then and now. Thank you for trying with my folks. In my own goofy way, I love you, kiddo."

"I love you, too. We've made a good team all this time. I'm gonna miss you."

"Only for a blink of an eye, Jos. I'll save you a place at the table."

He was gone. The machines shrieked and the sobs grew louder. Medical people came rushing in, but they couldn't save him. His devastated body had quit.

In the silence after the alarms were turned off and the sheet drawn over my friend's face, I approached his parents and the doctor.

"He wanted to be an organ donor, you know," I said. "He signed his license for it. He asked me to remind you."

His mother buried her face in her hands and drowned the wad of tissues she held. His father turned to me, eyes blazing.

"How dare you? You were supposed to be his friend and all you can think about is cutting him into little pieces?"

"What I'm thinking right now is my friend is gone and the last thing he asked me to do was to remind you of his wishes. I'm thinking he wants to help someone else with the organs he doesn't need anymore. And I'm thinking he must have told you about this in the past, since he asked me to remind you, not tell you about his wishes."

His father snorted. "And just how did he ask you all this? You weren't in the car with him."

"No, but I've been in this room with him for two days and we've carried on a long conversation during that time."

"You haven't said a word all these hours, Jocelyn. How have you conversed with him?" his mother asked as she lifted her face from the tissues.

"The only thing left working for him was his mind. He reached out to me and I heard him. We talked the whole time."

"What did he say to you?" she whispered.

"A lot of it was just remembering good times. But he gave me a couple more messages for you. He said he loves you and he's just gone on ahead. You'll be together again one day. He said he wanted good to come out of this, which is why he wanted me to remind you about the organ donation."

His father cut me off. "You could just be saying things you want. How do we know he had anything to do with it? I think you're very cruel to do this to us. You should leave now. And don't show up at his services. You won't be welcome."

The poor doctor had stood silent through the exchange, but he spoke up now.

"If your son signed to be an organ donor, we can honor his request. He was a legal adult. He can make a big difference in many lives. Why not check his wallet?"

"You're as bad as she is. A graverobber, that's what you are, a ghoul." His father's face reddened as his rage deepened.

"But, if it's what he wanted, darling, shouldn't we do it?" She put her hand on her husband's arm as her mouse of a voice fought through her tears. "Part of him would go on."

His father crumpled in the face of his wife's pain. "Fine, check his wallet. But if it isn't there, I will not allow my son to be butchered."

The eyes of everyone else in the room seemed to bore through me as the grieving father accepted his son's wallet from the nurse nearest the bedside table. I knew the moment he confirmed the donor signature by the way he straightened.

"As you say, he signed to be an organ donor. How could you know?"

"He talked to me inside my head, really. I guess you'd call it telepathy. He told me one more thing to tell you. He said, 'no more belly flops.' I'm not sure what he meant, but..."

"I do," he interrupted. A wisp of a smile crossed his face. "When he was learning to swim, he accidentally landed on his stomach when he tried to dive into the pool. He cried because it stung so much. I promised him it wouldn't hurt that way if he didn't do any more belly flops. I got him to laugh through his pain. It became our code word for getting through hurts."

"So, it was an important message?" I asked.

"The most important you could have delivered." He chuckled. "No more belly flops," he repeated and took his wife's hand. "What do we have to do, doctor, to make this happen for our son?"

I slipped from the room then, grateful I could fulfill his wishes. Oh, but it hurt to know he was gone. How could I go on without my dearest friend?

"No more bellyflops," echoed in my mind. "No more bellyflops," I whispered.

Poetry and Prose

By Vickie Hano Hawkins

Pondering Pumpkins

Autumn is here, a chill is near,
Sends shivers down my spine,
Pondering which pumpkin to choose
Among the dark green vines.

Big ones, small ones,
Orange, green, or white.
Which one shall I choose
To become my Jack O' Lantern tonight?

Don't want a silly crooked smile,
I will carve a mischievous grin.
The candle that burns inside you, pumpkin
Shall ignite my own fires within.

Pumpkin, come and chase away
My fears beneath the cold full moon.
It's Halloween, please keep me warm
From the chill of an ancient tomb.

I'll wrap you within my heavy shawl
As we pass under oaks in moonlight,
Where the hidden owls hoot warnings
"Beware of the dead tonight!"

Tomorrow folks in Louisiana will say,
"Blow out the pumpkin candles, chase the black cat away.
Let's adorn the graves of our loved ones
For this is All Saints Day."

Spears and Arrows

WHACK!

Chase slapped the mosquitos dancing around his face.

"Geez, I'll be counting turtle eggs in my sleep! That's if I *can* sleep tonight. My back feels like it's breaking. It must be a hundred degrees in the shade. Is there ever a breeze in Louisiana?"

He stretched his back, cracked his knuckles, then added, "I feel like I'm a hundred years old instead of seventeen."

"Will you stop your whining!" remarked Logan with a long southern drawl. "You complain more than anyone I've ever met."

Chase guzzled the last of his sports drink and readjusted his baseball cap.

"Sorry, Logan," he apologized to his cousin. "I didn't realize digging for turtle eggs is like working in an oven. It's a lot different than guarding sea turtle eggs on the beach."

Logan laid his shovel aside and sat on a stump before answering.

"Well, the owner of this reptile farm doesn't pay by the hour. He pays by the egg; or I should say, by the 'dozen.' You wanted to make a little money during your summer vacation. I pulled strings to get you this job for today. See if I ever help you again."

Chase wiped his face with the edge of his t-shirt.

"Cousin," he teased, "I'm here to bless you with my presence for a few more weeks. Afterward, I'll go home to St. Augustine Beach where there's always a breeze. I'll surf the waves, swim with dolphins, go deep-sea fishing. You know, normal stuff! You're a twenty-one-year-old Cajun man now. How come you're not a tour guide or alligator handler here? You planning to gather eggs until you croak like a bullfrog?"

Logan peered over his sunshades. Grinning, he picked up his shovel and stretched his tan muscular arms. He was six-foot-two and lean and sometimes he could play mean.

"Little cousin, you'd better watch yourself. I could wrestle gators if I wanted. It takes guts and smarts. I qualify, you bet. Besides, I have a second job at the bait shop. Saving up my money. Plan to open my own shop one day. Going to sell bait, supplies, food, and top-quality merchandise. I'll rent kayaks, too. But the only reason I let you help me out today is because my brother, Stevie, had to finish his driver's education classes this week. Otherwise, you'd be hanging out with him."

Chase gazed at the buckets of eggs he'd collected. "What kind of turtle eggs are these and what does the owner do with them?" he asked.

"There's a mixture of soft shell, red-eared slider, yellow belly, and maps. They incubate most of them here on the farm. Some are sold to other states. It's cool to watch the hatchlings grow," Logan replied.

"Seriously, Logan," Chase said, "do you ever have any fun? Can we go fishing tomorrow? I want to hunt for arrowheads at that spot on the river near your private landing. I'd like to watch you use your speargun, too."

Logan adjusted a wheelbarrow filled with plastic buckets of turtle eggs.

"Yeah, I guess so. I could spear some catfish. I need to restock the freezer anyway. Could sell a few, too. Make a little spending money. On top of that, we could fry some for dinner. Let's wrap it up and cash in our eggs. That's if you can walk or is your back broken from digging all day?"

Chase grimaced, thinking, *He treats me like a kid.*

But aloud he said, "I wish I could take a swim right now—even if it's in a muddy river and not the ocean."

"Yeah, well, just watch out for the gators," said Logan.

"Gators, sharks...it's all the same."

Logan shook his head in exasperation. "I'll drop you off at the house on my way to the bait shop. I'm sure Nanna's cooking up something good for dinner. Maybe I can finally have some peace and quiet."

* * * * *

Logan carefully tried to avoid the ruts and mudholes as he steered his Toyota Tacoma four-wheel drive, pulling boat and trailer. The dirt road meandered through the family property before sloping down at their private boat launch. It was a mere fifteen-minute drive from the house.

Their favorite fishing spot was located a few miles away off the main branch of the Tickfaw river. Once started, the twenty-horsepower boat motor whisked them away in the fourteen-foot flatboat.

Giant cypress trees stood guard over pristine waterways bordered by lily pads and cypress knees. Soon the two boys were enjoying a quiet summer afternoon. The hours crept by like a slow-flying crane.

Logan stood, spearfishing from the boat a short distance from the riverbank. His pneumatic speargun came equipped with a two-foot spear and twelve-foot ripcord. The water was shallow enough to show large fish, yet deep enough to swim. He caught six catfish weighing fifteen to twenty pounds each.

Chase fished with a cane pole from the opposite end of the boat saying, "I'm happy with the few fish I've caught. I'm going to swim to the riverbank now while you spear a few more. I'm ready to stretch and cool off. Need to find some arrowheads for my collection."

He slipped out of his shoes, then flung off his t-shirt and cap. He hastily attached the fishing line and large hook around his cane pole and tossed it on the bottom of the boat.

"Time to seek treasure," he said.

Logan took a drink from his water bottle, then wiped his face. "You be careful. You might have to fight the ghosts of our ancestors for that treasure."

Ghosts of our ancestors. Despite their "family feuds and ghosts in the armoire," Chase appreciated Logan's companionship. It was a miracle their families even associated with one another since the accident.

Would Logan be angry forever?

Chase dove off the flatboat to swim the short distance to the shore. He had waited all year to search for the Native American arrowheads. The afternoon sun baked his skin, but the water felt like heaven.

Reaching the swampy bank a couple of minutes later, he grasped onto cypress knees to help him climb up the slippery, muddy bank, hoping to find the perfect spearpoint.

Even a shard of pottery.

He needed to dig deep in the mud.

Darn. Left my pocketknife in the boat. Need a sharp stick.

Trudging through the mud in his bare feet, he reached for a good-sized branch, disturbing a tiny snake which wiggled away. Inhaling the earthy fragrance of the bayou, he dug, unearthing worms and tiny bugs.

It brought back childhood memories of digging for fishing worms with his dad and Uncle Walt.

Uncle Walt's been gone three years now...and Logan misses his dad.

The surface of the lazy river shimmered like diamonds. An egret flew by landing daintily amongst some lily pads. A bullfrog bellowed its presence. Time stood still in this paradise.

He kept digging.

Suddenly, Chase exclaimed, "Yes! I found one! What a beauty! This is the biggest arrowhead I've found yet! Just look at the color!"

He couldn't wait to show Logan. Tossing the branch aside, he slowly stepped into the river, wading, ready to swim to the boat.

The silence was broken by Logan's piercing scream, warning him of danger.

"GATOR! CHASE! WATCH THE GATOR! GATOR ON THE BANK BEHIND YOU!"

He had seen no sign of an alligator nest. But the female had been there hiding deep among the reeds and mud, guarding her precious eggs. Now she charged, hissing, displaying wickedly sharp teeth. Her armored hide was as tough and pointed as the prized arrowhead he dropped.

He gasped, held his breath, spun, and plunged headfirst into the river. Murky water raced through Chase's sinuses, burning clear to his brain. Fear ripped his heart.

His cousin's voice, muffled within the splashing and thrashing, was his only lifeline.

Every muscle jerked in his body as Chase swam toward the safety of the boat. His nerve endings braced for a death bite. He went under for a second. It seemed an eternity.

Not going to make it, he thought.

Was she going to pursue him this far from the bank? He couldn't stop to look back.

Please, God, help! he prayed.

Blazing sunlight glared off the water, burning his eyes.

Suddenly, he caught a glimpse of dazzling light reflecting from the tip of a spear. Logan stood in the boat, poised as he aimed the speargun in Chase's direction.

Would the spear hit its mark?

A fraction of an inch could be deadly—but for him or the *alligator*?

He thought he heard a shout—or was it the clicking release of the spear or the guttural moan of the gator?

Sloshing in a stinging whirlpool of panic, Chase glanced up to see his cousin's face.

Their eyes locked.

Logan's face was set in a cool, determined expression. This was a true test of a bayou warrior—a Louisiana sportsman. The spear shot over Chase's head and across the water.

Moments later, with Logan's help, he lay inside the boat in shock and exhaustion as his cousin wiped him down with a towel.

"Hey, you okay?" asked Logan.

Chase caught his breath and sat up.

"What happened? Am I dead? Where is it?"

"Ha! Ha! Ha! You should have seen the look of fear on your face. You survived the dance of death."

Chase regained his composure and glanced around, asking, "Did you kill the gator?"

Logan giggled then said, "Well, actually, the gator never followed you into the water. It's still over there on the bank. I think it was more interested in that egret than your skinny little..."

"What!" exclaimed Chase. "You let me believe I was about to die!" he retorted as he grabbed a bottle of water from the ice chest.

"Now, hold on just a minute. That gator was mad. She dashed toward you. Not to mention the water moccasin I saw swimming nearby. Yeah, I warned you. Probably saved your life. See if I ever help you again," Logan said.

Chase fumed and thought angrily, *I am so ready to go home!*

Logan turned to put away his speargun but as he stepped back, he screamed, not in joking but from severe pain, "AAAAGH!"

Chase quickly turned to see the large fishhook attached to his cane pole, now embedded in Logan's bare foot. He rose to help, accidentally stepping on the pole, jerking the line, causing the hook to tear deeper into Logan's flesh.

Blood oozed.

Logan cursed.

Chase acted swiftly. He quickly pushed the fishhook forward until the barb pushed through the skin. Opening the tackle box, he grabbed pliers and, using the wire cutter, snipped off the entire sharp end.

This allowed him to back the hook out without further tearing the wound. Dunking his discarded t-shirt into the crushed ice and water in the chest, he carefully wrapped the cloth around Logan's foot.

He started the boat motor and raced to the landing.

*   *   *   *   *

Ten minutes later, Chase helped Logan out of the boat to the truck.

"There's a first-aid kit under the passenger side seat. You get the boat while I take care of this mess," Logan said.

Chase quickly loaded the boat onto the trailer and secured their belongings. He cautiously approached Logan who was trying his best to stay calm, pain etched on his face.

"How you doing? Still bleeding?" asked Chase.

"Yeah, some. Stings like heck. I think I sprained my ankle, too. Let's get to the house. You drive," Logan replied as he leaned back in the passenger seat.

Suddenly, Chase realized he was now in another mess and his cousin would not be happy.

"Logan?"

"What, Chase?"

"Uh, I can't drive your truck."

Logan threw the first-aid kit on the floorboard in exasperation.

"Why not?"

Chase shuffled his feet and turned red with embarrassment.

"I shouldn't drive. I don't have a driver's license yet."

"What? Seventeen years old and no license?" Logan threw up his hands before grumbling, "Well, I certainly can't do it! Do you think you can drive this truck? We're on family land, not on a public road. No one around for miles. You can't run over anyone—or kill anyone."

Chase winced.

Why did he have to say that? I know what he's thinking. He hates me.

118

"Well, I don't know," stammered Chase. "Maybe I can. I've been paying attention. I drive the golf cart at home."

Logan tore open a packet of pain meds, grabbed a bottle of water from the console, then swallowed two pills. Taking a deep breath, he asked, "Chase, why don't you have a license yet?"

Adjusting his tennis shoes and hat, which he had retrieved from the boat, Chase focused on the crawfish mounds scattered across the field. "I'm afraid to drive because of the accident. I don't want it to happen again."

A black crow pranced around a puddle, then flew, settling in a live oak tree. It cawed as if it were telling the world it was boss of this bayou.

"Get in and I'll tell you what to do," Logan said. "It's easy enough. Just push in on the clutch, crank it up, and put it in gear. Then you'll ease up on the clutch and give it a little gas. I'll help shift. We can do this. Let's go."

* * * * *

Forty minutes later, after killing the motor numerous times and being jolted about as the gears tried their best to engage, they pulled into the driveway. Chase honked the horn, a long blast, something unusual.

Nana and Stevie stepped outside onto the porch of the old Acadian style farmhouse.

Chase killed the engine and jumped out of the truck yelling, "Nana! We've got to get Logan to the clinic. He might need stitches in his foot."

Nana took charge.

"Stevie, run inside and get that old pair of crutches from the hall closet. I'll get my car and drive him to town."

Ten minutes later, Nana and Logan were on their way to the clinic. Stevie turned to Chase and asked, "What happened to his foot?"

"He got in a fight with my fishhook," Chase said, trying to make light of the situation.

Stevie, being Logan's younger brother, knew things would be tense around the house later.

"If your fishhook picked a fight with Logan, I bet Logan's going to pick a fight with you when he gets home," Stevie said.

Chase sighed and replied, "I'd rather wrestle an alligator."

* * * * *

Two hours later Nana stepped inside the front door carrying a bag of prescription medications. Logan followed on crutches. He hobbled to his bedroom and slammed the door shut.

Chase sat in the kitchen, pushing aside a half-eaten sandwich before swallowing some iced tea. He grasped the bath towel draped around his neck, using it to dry his freshly washed hair. He inhaled the calming scent of fabric softener.

Nana walked into the kitchen and made herself a cup of coffee.

"How's Logan?" asked Chase.

"Oh, he'll live," she replied. "The doctor told him to stay off that foot for one to two weeks. Which means he won't be able to work. He's concerned he'll lose both of his jobs."

Chase rested his head on the table, hiding his face within the soft folds of the towel.

Nana sipped her coffee then asked, "Are you going to finish that sandwich?"

"No. I'm done," Chase mumbled into the towel.

Nana reached for the paper plate. "No need to let a good sandwich go to waste."

"I'm sorry, Nana. It was an accident. I didn't mean for it to happen," Chase said, as he cracked his knuckles and twirled the towel around his fingers.

Nana took a bite of the sandwich then cleared her throat. "Of course, it was an accident. We must make amends and go on."

Chase groaned and banged his fist on the kitchen table. "I just remembered the arrowhead. I found a beautiful arrowhead. But I lost it in the river. Never to be found again."

Nana chuckled. "Yes, Logan told me about your little adventure with the alligator."

Chased laughed. "I was never so scared in all my life. But you should have seen that arrowhead."

Reaching for her devotional King James Bible on the counter, Nana said, "You know what? The Bible teaches that children are like arrows."

"Yeah? How?" asked Chase.

Nana read the scripture aloud:

Like arrows in the hand of a warrior,
So are the children of one's youth.
Happy is the man who has his quiver full of them...

Psalms, Chapter 127, vs. 3-5

"I think it means it's a blessing and protection for a father, or mother, to have many children. I also believe it's a blessing to have only one child, too," she said.

Chase watched as Nana reached inside her Bible and pulled out a laminated copy of Uncle Walt's obituary. Nana caressed the notice and placed it back inside her Bible.

"You know, Chase, it's almost as if I lost two sons the day your Uncle Walt was killed in the automobile crash. It was an unavoidable accident. Your dad had to swerve off the road to avoid hitting a child. Walt was thrown from the passenger-side door and killed. Your dad has never forgiven himself for his brother's death. That's why he packed up and moved you and your mother to Florida. He just couldn't stand to live here and watch the boys and their mother grieve. He even signed over a part of his property to Logan and Stevie."

Chase wiped a tear from the corner of his eye and asked, "Do you hate my dad? Are you angry with us?"

Nana stood and walked over to Chase, wrapping her arms lovingly around his shoulders and kissing his cheek.

"No, I could never hate my darlings. I love you and your parents. We must learn to forgive one another and ourselves and go on with our lives," Nana whispered in his ear.

* * * * *

Chase rose early the next morning. He knew what he had to do.

"Where are you off to so early? Fishing?" asked Nana as she took a pan of freshly baked biscuits from the oven.

121

Chase selected two biscuits then took a small bottle of milk from the refrigerator.

"I'm going to be helping Stevie and his friends on a little project for the next week or so. His friend's dad is going to give us a ride every day. He's really happy to have some help."

Nana buttered biscuits then poured herself a cup of coffee.

"That sounds like a clever idea. Especially since Stevie's mom won't allow him to drive her car until he's added to the insurance policy. And you can forget about Logan offering anyone the opportunity to drive *his* truck."

Chase grimaced as he spread a spoonful of homemade preserves on a biscuit.

"Yes, a little work is just what you need, Chase. You'll stay busy making friends and you'll also stay away from Logan. Perfect!"

"Yeah, I figure Logan doesn't want me around right now. I wonder what he's going to do all day sitting around the house. He'll go crazy," said Chase.

Nana shook her hands in the air and said, "Oh! I told Logan he could help me paint and decorate my oyster shell ornaments. Why, Christmas will be here in about five months. I've got to prepare for the annual holiday craft fair. Also, his mom is planning on him to help shell butter beans from the garden. He can do it all sitting in a chair. Logan will be too busy to go crazy."

* * * * *

"Let's see. That's two bags of chips, three cold drinks, and a box of cold fishing worms. That comes to fifteen dollars and twelve cents," said Chase.

"How much are the fried gator bites?" asked the customer.

"Six dollars," Chase replied.

"Okay, give me some of those, too. That should do me for now," the customer added.

Mr. Rodrigue, the owner of the local bait shop, stepped out from the small kitchen in the back of the building. "This is the most gator I've sold in months, Chase. You're bringing me good luck. Or is it Voodoo? What's your secret?"

"It's no secret," said Chase. "I like to start up a conversation with customers. I tell them about that alligator I had to wrestle. Before you know it, all these Cajuns are hungry for some gator tail!"

"Are you sure you're not telling them fish tales instead?" Mr. Rodrigue asked jokingly.

He wiped his hands and brow with a camouflaged hand towel. "It sure is nice of you to fill Logan's spot for him while he's recuperating at home. I don't know what I would have done. But you stepped in and are doing a fantastic job."

"Thanks," said Chase. "I can't wait to see the look on Logan's face when I give him all my earnings and tell him he'll still have his job once I leave."

"You're not going to keep a little cash for yourself?" asked Mr. Rodrigue.

"Nope, not a penny."

"Just remember, Chase, you can eat all the gator bites and fried fish you want for free!"

* * * * *

Chase and Stevie waved good-bye as their friends pulled out of the driveway.

"Well, it's your last night here, Chase. Hope you had a fun time after all that's happened. My friends really like you. Especially Mr. Rodrigue."

Chase glanced down at the wooden case in his hands. "This made it all worthwhile. But now it's time to go inside and face Logan. Wish me luck."

Chase and Stevie quietly entered the house to find Logan resting in the recliner.

"Well, look what the cat drug in! Trouble times two," Logan stated sarcastically.

"How you feeling, Logan?" asked Chase.

"I'll tell you what. I'm about to go crazy sitting in this house. I don't want to see another oyster shell or butter bean ever again. First, my foot hurt. Now, my fingernails ache from shelling beans. My fingers burn from hot-gluing little fluffy balls on Nana's oyster shell ornaments. Give me a break!" exclaimed Logan.

Chase had to stifle the urge to laugh aloud. Not long ago, *he* was the one complaining about his *own* aches and pains.

"I have something to make you feel better, Logan," Chase said.

"What could you possibly have or do to make me feel better?"

Chase reached inside his pocket and pulled out an envelope, handing it to Logan.

"What's this?"

"Just open it."

Logan slowly unsealed the envelope and looked inside.

"What's this? Money?"

Chase couldn't help but grin.

"Yeah, and it's all for you, Logan. Over five-hundred dollars."

Nana and Stevie gathered closer to see.

"When Nana told me you wouldn't be able to work because of your injury and you were worried about losing your job, I wanted to help you. I asked Mr. Rodrigue if I could take your place at the bait shop until my vacation was over. I even managed to put in a few hours working at the alligator farm. Stevie did, too. I saved all my earnings for you."

"So that's what you've been up to," said Nana.

"Cousin, I can't take this money. You earned it, not me."

Chase put down the wooden case and tried to reason with Logan.

"I'm sure you probably don't need the money, Logan. Knowing you, you have stashed away tons of cash for a rainy day. But it's my way of saying thanks for saving my life. Besides, I was rewarded for all my hard work after all."

Chase pointed to the wooden case on the coffee table.

"Y'all come see what's inside."

Everyone gathered around as he slowly opened the lid. There on a bed of soft red velvet rested a collection of twelve perfectly pointed Native American arrowheads. Chase looked up as he heard them gasp in awe.

"Where did you find those?" asked Nana.

"They're a gift from Mr. Rodrigue. Want to know the best part? Mr. Rodrigue told me he and grandpa found these together when they were young. He's kept them all these years. He had them mounted in this cedar case. Logan, he also said they found these arrowheads near our favorite fishing spot," said Chase.

"I'm happy for you," said Logan. "But I'm not taking the money and that's final. Do you think you can just come back here and make everything okay again? My dad taught me to work for my own money. I don't like being a charity case."

Chase fumed. "Fine! But I'm never coming back here again."

He turned to leave the room.

"Good!" Logan shouted.

Nana grabbed Chase by his arm. "Wait! You stay right here."

She turned to Logan and said, "Young man, I think you'd better reconsider."

"Guys, please don't fight," Stevie pleaded.

A few moments passed. The room was filled with tension.

"Okay, okay!" Logan replied. "Chase, I expect to see you back here next summer. I need someone I can rely on to help me get my bait shop up and running."

"What about me?" asked Stevie.

Logan continued. "I'll need someone to drive and run errands for me."

Steve interrupted. "I can drive. Chase doesn't even have a driver's license yet. At least I have a permit..."

Logan interjected. "Stevie, no reason I can't have two partners."

He then turned to Chase and said, "I need someone with guts and a good head on his shoulders—someone to watch my back. What do you say?"

Smiling, Chase reached for Logan's hand. "Shake on it?"

"You bet," replied Logan, as he grasped his cousin's hand.

"Ouch! Dang it, Chase! You got a grip like a..."

"Like a gator?" asked Chase.

Logan grinned.

"Yeah. See if I ever help you again. Now, let's count this money together."

The End

Vickie Hano Hawkins

A Kindness Repaid

By Aaron Gordon

Mandy Mae had just come home from a 12-hour shift. She threw her scrubs in the hamper and jumped into the shower. She thought, "This hot shower feels so good!" After washing, she just stood, arms against the wall under the showerhead for at least five minutes. Then she turned the water off. She wrapped her body in one towel and her brown hair in another. All the curtains were drawn in her apartment, so she walked down the hall into her bedroom in her towels.

As soon as she walked into the small, square bedroom, she heard her cell phone ring in the kitchen. "Damnit," she said. She ran to the kitchen counter, almost losing her towel. She caught the phone on the last ring before voicemail.

"Hello?"

"Hello, this is Richard Lambert from Lambert and Lambert speaking. Is this Miss Trahan?"

"Speaking. Who are you again sir?"

"My name is Richard Lambert from Lambert and Lambert law firm. We have been entrusted with the care of the estate of a Mr. Pierre Gaudin. You have been named as a beneficiary of his estate."

"There must be some mistake, I never knew anyone of that name!"

"Miss Trahan, there is only one Mandy Mae Trahan in the entire parish. I am sure it is you. Do not be alarmed, as Mr. Gaudin's estate named several people who seem to have no connection with himself.

"Oh, I see. I have never inherited anything before, let alone from a stranger."

"Miss Trahan, when would be a convenient time to come down to our office at three three six North Eugene Street?"

"Well, I just got off work, how late are you in the office today?"

"We are here 'till five o'clock miss."

"Will you be available at four this afternoon."

"Yes, I am free for the entire afternoon."

"Very good sir, I will see you then."

Mandy Mae tapped the phone off, plugged it into her charger, and laid it on the counter. She filled up a plastic cup with water and made her way to the bedroom. With a sigh, she set her drink on her nightstand. She unwrapped the towel from around her body and slid her thin frame into bed. Before she could take a drink, she was fast asleep.

A loud honk from a truck awoke Mandy Mae with a start. She was groggy. As she came to her senses she glanced at the clock beside her bed. It read three thirty-seven.

"Crap!" Mandy jumped out of bed and frantically began to get dressed. She threw the towel off her head. Putting on underwear and a summer dress, she then ran to the bathroom. She dried and did her hair as fast as she could. She grabbed her concealer and haphazardly applied it to her face. A little powder on her nose, and some lip stain, and a quick dash of eyeshadow to match her brown eyes and dark complexion. That is the best she could do with the time she had. After having a quick pee, she washed her hands, ran down the hall and grabbed her purse, cell phone, and keys. She slammed the door shut and locked it. She looked at her phone. It read three forty-six. She was cutting it close.

When Mandy Mae arrived at the offices of Lambert and Lambert, she quickly pulled the door open and approached the reception desk slightly out of breath. The office smelled musty, like old wood.

"May I help you, miss?" The older lady behind the reception desk asked.

"Yes, I am here to see Mr. Lambert, um, Richard about an inheritance? My name is Mandy Mae Trahan."

"Oh yes. He is expecting you. He is finishing up with a client. Please have a seat. My name is Ms. Gertrude, can I get you anything to drink?"

Mandy sat down on a large brown leather sofa. She said, "Um, yes, I would love a glass of water please, Ma'am."

"Certainly, my pleasure." Ms. Gertrude gracefully pulled her plump backside from her chair and made her way to a doorway behind the reception desk. In a minute she returned and placed a glass of ice water on the mahogany coffee table in front of Mandy Mae.

"Thank you so much, Ma'am."

"My pleasure."

At that very moment, the door to the offices opened. A tall, gray-haired man in a suit bade farewell to a younger, blond man also in a suit. The younger man moved past the women out the front door with a nod of his head.

Ms. Gertrude turned to the gray-haired man. "Mr. Lambert, Miss Trahan is here to see you."

Mr. Lambert smiled, "Miss Trahan, please, please, follow me." Mandy Mae lifted her water and stood up. Mr. Lambert led Mandy May through the office door and down a small wood paneled hallway with several doors. The last door on the left was open. He walked inside and motioned for her to follow him. Inside the room was a very expensive looking desk with two sturdy wood chairs in front of it.

"Have a seat please, Miss Trahan." Mandy Mae sat down as Mr. Lambert walked and sat behind the desk. "Miss Trahan, we here at Lambert and Lambert deal with many cases of succession. You have been named a beneficiary of a specific item which is part of Mr. Pierre Gaudin's succession. Due to the nature of Mr. Gaudin's will, this item must be received by you, Miss Trahan before the rest of the succession can be distributed accordingly among the heirs."

"How strange. What does all this mean?"

"To put it plainly, you must receive this item and sign a document to take possession of it in order for us to move forward." Mr. Lambert began to lift a heavy object in a wooden box from the floor behind his desk onto the desktop.

"Why me? I never met or knew of anyone named Gaudin?" The item came to rest on the desk with a thud.

"I truly do not know. Perhaps he knew one of your parents or predecessors. Shall we begin?"

"Sure, go ahead." Mr. Lambert removed the top from wooden box and the sides as well. What appeared was a brilliant golden clock in the shape of an alligator head. The mouth was open, and the winding key was located inside the mouth at the back of the jaw. The clockface was on top of the gator's head. It, along with all the clockworks, were polished to a fine shine that sparkled with the reflection of the sun coming in through the office window. For a few seconds, not a word was spoken.

Finally, Mandy Mae spoke softly, "What is this? What is this? I never."

Mr. Lambert picked up a card from the rear of the clock and began to read it aloud, "Dear Trahan, though you may not know me, I know your family. In my youth, your family paid to me a certain kindness, which I now wish to visit on whomever still lives in the Trahan line. This is so important to me that I have held up my whole succession until it is received. Inside the clock is a ruby of substantial worth. Worth more than the clock itself. All you need do is wind the clock and it will be revealed. Please sign your receipt of this token of my appreciation for the Trahan family. Sincerely, Pierre Gaudin." Mr. Lambert put the card down. "All that is left is for you to sign for this, and then I can arrange for it to be brought to your apartment for you." He pulled out a folder with an official looking document in it. While he was retrieving a pen from his desk drawer, Mandy Mae spoke.

"I am shocked by this gift. It looks very complicated and expensive. I wonder how my family knew Mr. Gaudin?"

"Mr. Gaudin had a vast interest in the lumber industry. It could easily have been from his early years. He started out with almost nothing. Will you please sign on the line?"

"But of course." Mandy Mae signed the paper in beautiful cursive.

"Still," she said, "I am intrigued to see what ruby is inside. Although I am afraid to wind the clock. The alligator looks ready to eat."

Mr. Lambert responded, "I am sure it is quite fine. Odd, yes, but quite fine. Why not try winding the key?"

"Ok." Hesitantly, Mandy Mae stuck her small hand inside the gator clock and found the key at the back of the mouth. She tried to turn the key. At first, nothing happened. She then braced her arm on the desk and turned with more force. The key began to move. She could turn it slowly. The sound of the spring winding was loud. "Click. Click. Click. Click-Click." Suddenly, a began to open slowly on the back of the clock.

"Miss Trahan! It is working! I can see the stone! Keep going!"

Mandy Mae redoubled her efforts with a grunt. "Click. Click. Click. Click-Click. SNAP!"

"AAAAAAAAHHHHH!" Mandy May screamed as the jaws of the gator snapped shut on her slim hand. Blood began seeping out of the clock onto the desk.

"Good Lord! GERTRUDE! COME QUICKLY!"

Gertrude bounded down the hallway with several thuds before turning into Mr. Lambert's office.

"AIIIEEEEEE!" She screamed when she saw the ghastly sight. Mandy Mae's blood had begun to spill over the desk onto the floor. Her left hand was bloody as well from trying to pry open the mouth of the clock. "Sweet Mary and Joseph!"

Mr. Lambert's hands were beginning to bleed from trying to assist opening the jaws. "Gertrude! Bring me the toolbox from the closet and then call an ambulance!"

"Yessir!" Gertrude thudded quickly down the hallway and quickly back with the toolbox. While Mr. Lambert rummaged in the toolbox, Gertrude picked up the phone and dialed emergency services.

"Yes!" Mr. Lambert pulled a small cat's paw from the toolbox and attempted to pry open the golden clock jaws. He felt thankful to God when the jaws began to separate.

* * * * *

Long after the ambulance had taken Mandy Mae to Baton Rouge General for treatment, Mr. Lambert finished up his statement to the police detective in his office. A black-haired man in a sportscoat with a thick mustache was taking notes on a pad of paper as he listened. The detective didn't look up as he asked his question.

"Mr. Lambert, what happened next?"

"Well, Detective, after we managed to extract Miss Trahan's hand from that infernal machine, Ms. Gertrude wrapped her hand tightly in a clean rag. Then we both helped her out to the lobby, where the paramedics were just coming through the door. They saw to her and took her away on a stretcher."

"And then what happened?"

"Shortly afterward, a police car and a firetruck pulled up. The officers asked some questions, and then taped off the scene until you arrived."

"I see. And can you tell me any more about what was in the back of the clock?"

"I saw a rather large looking ruby in there. But I didn't have time to examine it."

The detective sighed. "Thank you for your cooperation, Mr. Lambert. I'll come back in the morning to finish up the investigation, and unless something comes up, you should be able to have your office back."

"Thank you, detective."

"Sure. Thank you for your cooperation. There is only one thing that won't leave my mind. Perhaps you know what it means."

"What are you talking about, detective?"

"In the clock, behind the ruby there was an inscription. It read: Thank you for the limp. Consider that kindness repaid."

Prose

By Brenda Birch Gallaher

What an Adventure We Had

"I'm off to Lisa's," I announced as I popped into the kitchen. My mother was making her second pot of coffee, its aroma warm and exotic.

"Hold on, when will you be back?" my mother asked, leaning into the fridge. Her voice was muffled.

I shrugged my shoulders. I knew she would shorten whatever time frame I gave her. "I don't know. When do you want me back?"

We must have been out of half-n-half because my mother put milk on the table for her coffee. She closed the door and looked at me. "It's already ten, so be back by 1:00 p.m."

"Yes, ma'am," I answered as I turned and headed for the front door.

"And put on a sweater. It's too cold to go outside like that."

"Yes, ma'am," I said without looking back at her. I returned to the bedroom I shared with my sister and pulled a dark blue sweater out of the closet. I put it on as I headed for the front door. I walked down our long driveway, past my mother's blue Chevy station wagon, and on to Lisa's. I had freedom for a few hours.

Lisa's house was much better than mine. One, it wasn't my house, two, she was half a block from the Humane Society filled with kittens and puppies, and three, the back wall of her fence bordered a horse riding stable. We would sit on the wooden fence and watch people ride in and out on big, beautiful tan or black horses. I hoped today was one of the days we fence sat.

Lisa's five year old sister, the one with the constantly runny nose, answered the door and let me in. I found Lisa in the kitchen washing breakfast dishes.

As usual, her older brother sat at the kitchen table reading a comic book. I picked up a kitchen towel and started drying. Lisa was pale, thin, had medium-brown hair, blue eyes, crooked teeth, and a contagious laugh. She fidgeted a lot, and nearly broke several plates on the edge of the sink.

"What is wrong with you? You got ants in your pants?"

"No, I got a great idea, but I want to wait until it's just the two of us," she whispered as she looked over my shoulder at her brother.

I looked at him also, and wondered if he was trying to listen in on our conversation.

What kind of trouble are we in for this time? I wondered.

We finished the dishes, drained the sink, and went to her bedroom.

Lisa jammed a chair under the door knob for privacy. This is what really made me nervous. What did she have to tell me? Sometimes her schemes didn't turn out so well. At times I felt I was auditioning for an Abbott and Costello movie.

We sat on her bed.

Lisa's room was half the size of the one I shared with my sister. Her room contained one double bed her two little sisters shared, and a single bed for her. Three mismatched chests of drawers engulfed the rest of the room.

My bedroom, on the other hand, was quite large. Karen and I both had single beds, our own closets, and a chest of drawers each. The one thing the two rooms had in common was the mess and clothes strewn everywhere.

"What's so important you don't want anyone to hear?"

Lisa looked at the door and back to me, whispering, "Can you ride a horse?"

"Nope," I used my normal voice and looked at her sideways. "Why?"

"Shh... I used to ride all of the time before we moved here, but we had to sell my horse. There just wasn't money for it."

"That's just mean, but what does that have to do with me, and if I can ride a horse or not?"

I waited for her answer. *Now* it didn't seem like such a good idea to sit on the fence and watch the horses come and go. Then I thought how cruel it was of her parents to sell her horse and move behind a riding and boarding stable.

"I was thinking maybe the owners would let us muck stalls in exchange for free rides," she said, pausing for dramatic effect as she leaned closer to me.

She had the broadest smile and a look of victory on her face as she sat back.

"What does *muck stalls* mean?"

Lisa's face fell.

"I told you I can't ride. Why'd you think I'd know anything else about horses?"

Lisa bounced a little on the edge of the bed.

"Okay, guess you're right," she said, sighing. "Mucking a stall means shoveling poop and dirty hay out. We could-"

I didn't let her finish. "You want to do *what*? I don't even clean up after the stupid dog, and now you want me to clean up after a horse!"

"It would probably be more than one horse. We'd have to muck several stalls in the morning, depending on how many they keep there."

I could feel my lips draw down in a frown, and that's how the adventure began.

Lisa wanted to ride again, didn't want to do it on her own, and asked me - her best friend - to join her.

After a little more coaxing from her, we agreed we'd get our parents' permission before we talked to the owner.

Looking back, we had a lot of chutzpah for two thirteen-year-olds, thinking we could go up to this big burly man and make a deal with him. We would each muck three stalls in exchange for riding free. To Lisa, it was heaven. To me, it was too much work.

But our parents decided it was okay, so that's what we did. It would be summer soon, and we needed something to do.

Our next step was to talk to the man who ran the place. We were both petrified and giddy with delight at the same time, so much so, it took us a week to gather our nerves and walk over. Of course we had to go the long way, we couldn't just jump over the back of her fence. The walk frayed our nerves even more. It was April by then, and the mornings were crisp instead of cold. The sky was blue and cloudless, and as we watched someone ride away we could see the horse's breath as it exhaled. We were dressed in jeans and sweatshirts; mine was burgundy and hers was yellow.

When we arrived at the office, the owner and his son sat on the porch drinking coffee. Lisa stuttered several times before she got out what she wanted us to do in exchange for riding free. The son glared at us. The father, the one who would make the decision, listened to us. His answer wasn't no, but it wasn't yes either.

Once he received permission from our parents, we could start the following Saturday at 8:00 a.m., when they put the horses out into the corral. We should be there at that time and be prepared to work.

"And to work hard," his son added.

His father ignored him.

Before we left, we each wrote down our parents' names and telephone numbers. Our spirits were a little higher than before entering the stable grounds.

The following Saturday morning was our first time cleaning out horse stalls. Lisa knew what to do, but I didn't.

The owner walked us over to the stable, and I nearly fainted from the stench. Here I thought my brothers' farts were disgusting and could curdle milk, but this was a thousand times worse.

He gave us each a pair of old, beige colored but dirty gloves to put on. Then he handed us each a shovel.

I'm sure I looked scared.

Mr. Hancox rolled a large red, but rusted wheelbarrow over to the first empty stall, opened the gate and pushed it in. I decided not to eat breakfast before next week's visit.

He dragged a wheelbarrow over for Lisa. "When you are finished, come to the office and get me," he said.

Lisa said yes, but all I could do was nod my head. I was afraid if I opened my mouth I would vomit. On the other hand Lisa was giddy, and I was ready to commit murder.

"What did you get me into?" I crossed my arms.

"What do you mean? This will be fun. Just think of riding for free."

"It's not free if we have to shovel poop and pee."

"Okay, but let's get to work," Lisa said as she ignored my obvious pain, the pain of rancor and hard work.

She entered her stall, and I had no choice but to do the same. I held my breath, entered my stall, and scooped up a large shovel full of poop. It had the consistency of barely firm pudding. At that point I wasn't sure I could eat chocolate pudding again. I was completely grossed out.

That first morning took us hours to shovel poop and wet hay. After we got a wheelbarrow full, we'd roll it over to a large wooden box, using the shovel to scrape it out. Until then, the hardest work I had ever done was to load a U-Haul truck, but that was nothing compared to the backbreaking work of shoveling horse waste.

After several hours of grueling work, we signed out and went home.

I barely made it to my bed before I fell into a deep sleep. The next thing I knew, Lisa jumped on the bed and startled me awake. Although I had slept for several hours, it felt as if I had just closed my eyelids.

"Let's go."

Her smile made me homicidal.

I rolled off the bed and got up. We, or I, dragged my half-dead carcass back to the horse stable.

She jumped and skipped all the way there. This made me more homicidal.

I put on a fake smile and happy face before entering the office.

Mr. Hancox already had horses saddled for us. Because I was a novice rider, he gave me a very docile horse. The horse he set up for me was so large, John Wayne would have needed a ladder to get on it; I used a fence rail.

It took all spring and the beginning of summer, but I learned to ride and control the horse, and therefore have a good time.

One morning in mid-June felt different. There was something in the air, and that usually meant Lisa was up to something.

We signed in, went over to the barn, put on our rubber outer shoes, and grabbed a shovel and pair of gloves. All but one horse was either out with its owner or in the large corral. The one remaining was pregnant, and we were told to stay away from her.

We threw our shovels into wheelbarrows and dragged them over to our selected stall. The heated poop made my nose curl at the stink, and I did my best not to vomit. At eight o'clock in the morning, the temperature was already in the upper-eighties. The heat made us work faster. The sooner we finished cleaning the stalls, the sooner we could go home for a bath and nap before returning in the afternoon.

It was not unusual for us to go to the far back corral, which we found through exploration, to watch the donkeys, mules and the one zebra ignore each other. The zebra is what would be referred to as an "attractive nuisance."

I have always been fascinated by zebras, so I was quite delighted to see one up close. I love their unique markings, as no two are the same.

Lisa climbed on the fence, and I followed her. "Hey, wanna ride the zebra?"

Without hesitation I answered, "You know I do. But I don't think Mr. Hancox will let one of us take it this afternoon.

I sighed. I really wanted to ride the zebra.

"Not this afternoon. I mean *now.*"

"We aren't supposed to bother him in the mornings. We do our work, come back in the afternoon, and ride. A horse, not a zebra. He won't saddle the zebra for us."

"I swear."

"That's nothing new."

"Don't be a smart ass," she huffed. "I mean we can ride bareback like they do in all of those Western movies you watch."

I almost fell off as I grabbed the fence and whipped around to look at her. "You're crazy!" I declared.

"Maybe, but I still wanna ride the zebra. If you're too chicken..." She smiled at me.

"You know I'm not chicken. It's just..."

"Just what?"

"Well, your ideas tend to get us into trouble, or at the very least, into hot water."

"Like what?"

"Setting the mouse trap with peanut butter. Tying your little sister to the clothesline like she was Joan of Arc."

"Never mind that. My stupid brother told me to do those things. Now, do you want to ride the zebra or don't you?"

"Yes, but," I started saying as I shook my head, afraid of the trouble she would start.

Lisa jumped into the corral, and like the best friend I was, I jumped down off the fence after her.

We went to the right side fence where she grabbed the lasso hanging on a post, and slowly walked towards the zebra. She caught it, walked it back over to me, and handed me the rope before she climbed up the fence.

"Hold its neck. I want to get on."

With as much bravado as a seventh grader could muster, I got closer to the zebra, and put my right arm around its neck. Its hair was soft, but warm from the sun as I laid my cheek on its cheek. I held the fence with my free hand.

Before Lisa sat on its back, she took the rope from me, and I watched as she sat.

I let go.

The zebra took off like a wild steer at a rodeo, and Lisa was on the ground in less than two seconds. She landed flat on her back as her ride ran away with the rope trailing behind it, whipping up dust.

I ran over and kneeled next to her.

Her eyes were closed.

I shook her shoulder, and she sat straight up.

"*WOW!*" was all she could say. She slapped at her clothing, and dust flew everywhere.

I waved my hand in front of my face at the ascending dirt.

She jumped up.

"Your turn," she said with glee.

I got up and backed away from her. "You're really crazy! You lasted all of one second."

"Not true," she responded, and stood a little straighter as she adjusted her clothes. "I counted, and I lasted two seconds."

"You're splitting hairs."

"Who cares? It's your turn."

"You mean my turn to die? Just because it didn't kill you, doesn't mean I should give it a chance to kill me."

Just how hard did you hit your head on the ground? I wondered to myself.

Lisa flashed me one of her mischievous grins. "So then, you *are* chicken! Do you have a big yellow streak down your back, too?"

I shoved her. "I'm neither afraid nor chicken."

I wanted her to know I was neither, just in case there was a difference. "Get that zebra back over here, I'll take my turn."

I headed for the fence as my stomach flopped in apprehension.

Lisa ran after the zebra, which was stupid, because it ran. This caused me to wait longer to take my turn, which gave more time for my stomach to be queasy. My heart raced, my hands got sweaty, which I blamed on the heat, and my mouth went dry.

I climbed the fence and waited for Lisa to bring the beast back.

It snorted, balked, and its ears laid flat against its head. It eyed me as if I was a one bite snack. I swallowed hard, wiped the sweat off my forehead, and ignored my thoughts of running home. Lisa smiled at me as she turned the zebra so I could climb on. She held its neck, but continued to smile and bounce on her feet.

"Anytime you're ready, *Chicken Little.*"

I hated her at that moment. On several occasions, I had mentioned to her that she caused more mischief than a Leprechaun, and *they* included a pot of gold. Lisa's gold pot was empty and smelly.

I closed my eyes, counted to ten, inhaled, and exhaled slowly. I was doing anything I could to waste time before getting on the zebra. Although I had always wanted to ride a zebra, I was sure there was a good reason why I had never had the opportunity in the past.

I took another deep breath, exhaling slowly trying to calm my jittery nerves, stood up on one of the fence railings, and announced with a trembling voice, "Okay, I'm ready. Hold'er still."

Lisa's smart mouth almost undid me. "It's a boy." Her smile got bigger.

"*Whatever.* Just hold it still."

Lisa held the zebra's neck, leaned against the fence, and nodded to me.

I grabbed the short stubby mane with my left hand, held onto the fence with my right before I put my leg over its back, and sat.

I instantly regretted not being a chicken.

Lisa let go before I was ready.

It bucked across the corral, sending the other animals scattering out of its way. It bucked me three or four times before I flew off, rolling to a stop facedown. Movement was impossible due to the wind that had been knocked out of me. I had no idea of what to do next. *Now* I understood why Lisa had just laid there after being thrown.

Dirt sprayed around my body as Lisa ran to me and squatted.

"You did wonderful," she squealed. "I bet that was a good five seconds before you hit the ground."

I gingerly rolled to my side and opened one eyelid.

In spite of the pain, I tried to give her the evil eye. Instead, I ended up laughing hysterically. Thirteen years old, and I had done something neither of my parents nor any of my siblings had ever done. *I* had ridden a zebra. Yeah, it was for only four or five seconds, but I had actually ridden a zebra.

Lisa jumped up, grabbed my hand, and helped me to stand up straight.

The pain in my side made me wish she'd left me lying there. We looked at each other and then ourselves, and no matter how much slapping at our clothes we did, there was no way we were getting rid of all of the dirt.

We laughed and pushed each other as we limped back to the fence we had originally climbed over.

As we hit the ground on the other side, Mr. Hancox came around the old tack building. He walked at a quick clip.

"What have you two been doing?" he said as he looked at both of us.

"I wanted to pet the zebra and the donkeys and the mules," I answered innocently, but I refused to look him directly in the eyes.

He looked at me, then at Lisa, and then back at me. "You girls stay out of that corral! Is that understood?"

He stepped closer.

We both nodded.

It felt like a hundred bees buzzed in my head, and I had blurry vision.

His son called to him, and before he trotted back to the office he said, "Stay out of that pen."

I grabbed Lisa's arm to steady myself. Once I caught my breath, we each limped on a different leg back to the office. We were covered in dirt and needed a bath, but we didn't care.

On this day we accomplished something other than moving poop and pee from one spot to another.

A sense of triumph filled our young hearts, and I found out something about myself. I discovered I can do what I set my mind to, with a little pushing from my best friend.

What an adventure we had that day!

The End

First published in *Manchac Review,* Vol.5, Southeastern Louisiana University, 2017.
Awarded 2nd place in the new voice category for the League of Utah Writers Annual Writing contest in 2017.

Front and Center

Sharon's smile was fake and she knew it.

She was so sick of attending wedding after wedding after wedding and it was never her turn. Here she was, forty years old, and never married. In her twenties and earlier thirties she was always in the bridal party.

Now she was just an invited guest, but it was her own fault. She was an attorney who worked seventy hours a week and had just been made a partner in her law firm. She was quite sure the job just wasn't worth it anymore.

"Okay," Leslie, the bride, said. "Everyone get together in front of the water fountain. I want one big shot of everyone."

People slowly gathered around the water fountain, mostly in couples, as they awaited instructions from the professional photographer.

Really, she thought, when will it be my turn?

Although it was a beautiful July afternoon with soft willowy white clouds passing overhead and a light breeze, Sharon groaned in her head, keeping the fake smile plastered on her face.

At six foot tall, Sharon always stood in the back of any group photo.

For once, she would love to stand in the front. All of the group pictures she ever had taken showed only her face or face and shoulders.

She moved to the back of the fountain in the center of the group.

A man joined her. He was taller than she was.

He extended his hand saying, "Hi, I'm Mark. I'm the groom's cousin."

Sharon accepted his hand. Her hand fit nicely into his. This was unusual because she had large hands.

"I'm Sharon. The bride is my first cousin, once removed."

Not only was Sharon tall, but to Mark she looked like a Greek goddess, with her light blonde hair and pale blue eyes, the opposite of him. Mark had dark brown hair, deep blue eyes and a dimple in his right cheek.

"I'm glad to know there's someone to stand at the back of the group picture with," he said. "I don't know about you, but I'm tired of being the tallest person and having to be in the back all the time. For once, I'd like to stand in the front, or even sit on the ground in the front."

143

Sharon's mouth gaped open.

Did I just hear him correctly? Is there another person who hates standing in the back, like a forgotten broken toy?

She gulped. "I know exactly what you mean. Ever since seventh grade I've had to stand in the back. It's like I'm being punished for my genetics."

Mark's laugh was so loud, everyone at the wedding turned to look at him. He and Sharon ignored the others.

"That's exactly what I said to my father. He told me to grow up."

"Did you tell him that's what the problem was? You'd already grown up above everyone else's height."

"Yes. He grounded me for a week for being smart."

A laugh escaped Sharon. She liked this man.

"I guess I should tell you what I do for a living before we go too far. A lot of people are turned off by it."

"You're a pole dancer at the local strip club?"

He bounced on his heels and smiled with only the left side of his mouth. He dug his hands deep into his pants' pockets.

Sharon's smile dropped and her eyebrows tried to reach each other.

Then his smile broadened, making her think of an elf about to cause mischief.

She gasped anyway. "Uh, no. I'm an attorney. I work 60-80 hours a week, and I just made partner."

Mark threw his head back this time when he let out his loud roaring laugh. It made Sharon's smile return.

"I'm an attorney, too. I run my own one-man firm helping the less fortunate."

"So you rarely do anything spontaneously?" Sharon sighed.

"On the contrary. One time, I suddenly had four days off and hopped the next open seat to Edinburgh, Scotland. It was the best trip ever."

"I haven't done anything *that* spontaneous. The best I could do was skipping school to go shopping."

Before she could say anything, Mark grabbed her hand, pulling her around the group of people gathering for pictures and down onto the grass in front of everyone.

Her frilly dress flew up as she sat, but she didn't bother to straighten it.

"Here we'll sit and be front and center," he said as the impish smile returned.

The bride gasped, bending over and patting her cousin on the head.

Sharon looked up to see Leslie's eyes were wide with shock.

"What are you two doing?" she chided. "You need to be at the back of the group."

Sharon sat up a little straighter, "We're tired of being relegated to the back of pictures because of how tall we are. For a change, we'll be in the front of a group picture."

"Everyone look at me please!" the photographer said, making the final adjustments on his camera.

"Never mind," Robin said, taking his bride by her hand. "Let them sit there."

Pulling his new wife to his side, he wrapped his arms around her waist.

"I'm going to count to three, so everyone get ready," the photographer said.

Sharon and Mark looked at each other, put their heads close together, and smiled big for the camera—front and center!

The End

First published in *Manchac Review,* Vol.4, Southeastern Louisiana University, 2016.

Notes, and More Notes...

By Vicky Fannaly

The day started out like any other day, except for the note. Nipper, my rat terrier, was peacefully gnawing on it, leaving a trail of tiny fragments on the rug. I traded a piece of breakfast sausage for the soggy piece of paper. Probably something of value like a hearing aid advertisement, I surmised. Opening it carefully, I was surprised to read "at the Corner Café, noon today."

Who had sent me this? Nipper finished eating her bribe and was sniffing at the bottom of the door. Was that where the paper had come from – was it slipped under the front door? Nipper looked with longing at the paper in my hand. Surely, she had not had it long.

Was I curious enough to go to the Corner Café at noon? Who would have sent a note instead of just calling me on the phone? The possibilities were few. I was curious, thrilled, and apprehensive, all at the same time. Perhaps there was more to the note that would have explained it, but the remnants were well chewed by Nipper.

I live in a very friendly community called Ponchatoula, LA. The residents sprawled out in new subdivisions in all directions from the quaint main street stores. Most were driven north from New Orleans by the hurricane devastation to that city. Many people commute to Baton Rouge, New Orleans, or to the many industrial plants along the Mississippi River. They enjoy the peaceful country atmosphere on the weekends.

It was almost noon, and I had nothing better to do but check out the invitation I had just received. I was a bit intrigued and admittedly bored enough to go. I ran a comb through my short dark hair, which I thought made my diminutive stature look taller. Dressing quickly so I wouldn't be late, I drove the mile to the main street and parked along the railroad tracks, which run north and south through the parish.

On the way to a vacant table, I saw the mayor and his wife, who greeted me cheerfully. I stopped to chat with several people from church who were enjoying crab corn chowder and salad or layered sandwiches. No one acknowledged sending me a note.

I sat where I could view both entrances. I was a bit early, so I ordered coffee and some beignets, a treat associated with the New Orleans coffeehouses - Café Du Monde and Morning Call. These were smaller take-offs: bite sized and filled with Bavarian cream. I was licking the remnants of powdered sugar off my fingers when Kathy, the owner, came over with a note. Not again, I thought.

"This came for you earlier, but I didn't see you when you came in," she said.

"Who left it?"

"I'm not sure. Someone left it at the counter. I didn't see who."

Sure enough, my name was on it with an instruction to deliver it to me when I arrived at noon. Baffled, I tore the envelope open. At least this note was intact: "Was not able to meet for lunch, see you tonight."

Again, no name! This was beginning to feel creepy. Did I really want to meet my anonymous note writer? My mind turned over places I could go, but that would just delay what seemed inevitable. The writer knew where I lived as they left a note there earlier.

Time to call for backup! My friend Lydia was just the person. She was levelheaded in a crisis, resourceful, and able to cut through smoke and mirrors. Lydia was even shorter than I was. Her hair was red currently but had been a few other colors in the past. She had an innate sense of mischief that made her a valuable ally in an adventure.

That evening, Lydia and I had just finished an elaborate Chinese takeout dinner when the knock sounded. Our cars were inside the garage and not visible. We both tensed as I asked who was there. Alas, no peephole in the door. I made a mental note to install the one I had purchased last year but had not installed yet.

"It's Bob! Weren't you expecting me?"

Bob, my long lost, not missed, ex-husband, walked in when I opened the door.

"Why didn't you call me instead of leaving notes with no name?"

"Broke my cell phone. Didn't you recognize my handwriting? I'm in a jam and need your help."

"Hey, I'm all tapped out."

"Don't look at me," Lydia chimed in.

"No, I don't need money, but I need a place to stay for a few days," Bob said as his phone clipped on his belt, began to ring.

"I thought you said your phone was broken. Aren't you going to answer it?"

"My line might be tapped. I need to stay somewhere no one would look for me. Everyone knows our history. Who would believe you'd take me in?"

"What makes you think I will?"

"Because you would not want the father of your children thrown to the wolves, would you? Think of little Robbie and Tina."

"Bob, we didn't have children, remember? That was your second wife, and those are your stepchildren."

"Please help me," he begged, looking so pitiful I started to contemplate doing it.

"Oh, give me a break," Lydia said, rolling her eyes. "You're not really considering it, are you?"

"I need to know what's going on – whom are you hiding from this time?"

"My girlfriend Patty's brother."

"No-neck Nick, your bookie? Why is he after you? Do you owe him money?"

"Much worse, I took a flash drive over with family photos that Patty made. Somehow, I picked up the wrong flash drive when I left. It was one of Nick's personal ones. I didn't get a chance to see what was on it, but it must have been really incriminating. He found out and wants it back. I was going to make a copy on my computer and try to slip it back, but Patty caught me. She told him."

"Why would Patty do that?"

"She caught me in bed with her sister. You know how women throw themselves at me. I didn't make the first move."

I tried not to laugh, but Lydia was laughing so hard that soon we were both making Bob angry.

"Lydia, you yourself know how good I am as a lover!"

That stopped both of us! When Bob left me for his second wife, he never returned to Ponchatoula. That could only mean one thing! He had to have been cheating on me with Lydia while we were married. Lydia was my very best friend – until now.

"I think you both need to leave right now," I said, feeling very empty and cold inside.

"But it was only a few times," Bob whined.

Too much information. I picked up Lydia's purse and sweater and put them on the porch, then pushed them both outside despite their protests. I was numb with shock to think that my best friend had hidden her relationship with my then husband from me. Bob, I could understand. He was always a rotten dog. I was too cold inside to cry, but a rage came over me that made me want to hate them.

Suppose they came back? Lydia knew where my spare key was kept. I went outside to retrieve it from over the door frame. I did not want them to come inside while I was away. I reached and felt the key and something I had not put there – a flash drive! Bob was up to his old tricks!

I spent a restless night going over all the time Lydia and Bob could have been together. It was hard to put out of my mind. An image of them laughing tortured me. I wished they would both disappear!

The following day when my rage cooled from sizzling to white hot, I went to visit a friend who was home bound. I put Bob's flash drive over her doorsill where no one would think to look. We drank coffee and spent a few hours chatting about things we had discussed many times. She enjoyed repeating them, and it passed the time. My fury over Bob and Lydia did not make me a gifted conversationalist.

Eight days passed and I was still fuming about Lydia and Bob. I was angrier at her than at him because I knew he was a lying dog and would never change. With her, I guess I expected more. But even I had succumbed to Bob's charming ways, so how could I expect more of her?

I was at Rouse's grocery, sale paper in hand, when I met one of my friends, Sue, from the garden club.

"Hey," she said, "I've been looking for Lydia all week. Have you seen her? I called and even went to her house. She's supposed to be my co-hostess at the next garden club meeting."

My heart sank! What had I wished for - that Lydia would disappear? Surely it was not so? Guilt overtook my ill feelings for my former friend. I chatted very briefly with Sue and left without buying anything. Lydia lived in a rural section, and she could have fallen on her property and be lying helpless, unseen.

I do not remember the drive there, but I was praying that nothing had happened to my best friend. I retracted all the bad thoughts and evil things I had wished on her. The truth was that I would be heartbroken if she were no longer in my life. Even Bob, miserable cur that he was, would always have a soft spot in the back of my heart. I prayed they were all right.

When I got to her house, I called her name as I rushed to the door. She kept her spare key over the door also - excellent hiding place when that is the first place one would look. It was missing! I tried the doorknob. The handle turned easily; it was not locked! Praying I would not find Bob and Lydia in a clinch, I opened the door. Looking inside, I saw that the place had been trashed - even more so than Lydia usually kept it.

I did not want to go inside in case someone evil was still there, so I went around the windows to check for Lydia. The rooms appeared empty. I called the sheriff's office and waited in my car until they came. I explained that my friend, whom I had last seen a week earlier, was missing, and the house looked like it had been ransacked. No, I did not want to go in to look.

The deputy was gone only a few minutes and returned to fill out his report. I gave him a description and a picture of Lydia from my wallet. I told him I had last seen her at my house, omitting the unpleasant visit from Bob. I felt numb and do not remember much about the deputy's interview. As soon as I could, I left, sorting my feelings all the way home.

Perhaps Bob was right, maybe No-Neck Nick was after him. Maybe I should go on a trip somewhere. After all I was the one who had the flash drive. I wondered what was on it. I should have looked before moving it to another doorsill. I needed to retrieve it, but the first thing I needed to do was pack and vacate my house.

When I got home, I hurried inside, stopping short in the living room. A nice-looking man was sitting on my couch with Nipper happily in his lap. I tried to appear calm and wondered if I had left the door unlocked. Fear and rage competed, as I struggled to calm my voice which still trembled as it squeaked at him.

"How did you get in?"

"Used your spare key under the flowerpot – first place I looked. Most people put it over the door sill," he said smugly as he rubbed Nipper's ears. If the traitorous dog were a cat, she would have been purring loudly by now.

"I have the police on speed dial," I said, whipping out my phone.

"I don't think you want to do that. Bob and Lydia could be in serious trouble. The police would just increase their problems."

"Did you trash Lydia's place? What were you looking for?"

"I didn't do that, but I got there shortly afterward. Of course, if you don't care what happens to them..."

I hesitated. Why should I care? Just because Lydia stayed with me when I had my appendix operation and needed help? Then there was the time my car broke down on the way back from the Gulf Coast and I was stranded. It was Lydia to the rescue even though it was three a.m. Maybe because I was wild about Bob when we were young and hot for each other – was that reason to care?

"Why shouldn't I call the police?"

"I can help you find Lydia, and I can help them out of their dilemma."

"And what exactly is their 'dilemma?'"

"Bob Williams has a flash drive that Nick Guzzardi wants back. He is willing to be very rough to get it back. Bob called his mother on Lydia's land line. Nick had Mrs. Williams' line tapped. His guys missed Bob but tossed the place looking for the flash drive."

I was feeling a bit weak in the knees. I needed to pack and get out of my house quickly.

As if he read my mind, my uninvited guest suggested I throw some things together and go to a friend's house. Why should I trust him? I did not even know his name or what he did.

"My name is Jim Bradford," he said and handed me a business card. "I was hired to find Bob and get the stolen flash drive."

Dang! He was a mind reader.

"Who hired you?"

"Sorry, client confidentiality. But if I were you, I would get out fast. Can I take you somewhere? Oh, I found a note on your door when I got here."

As I read the note, he passed to me, I had to smile. It said, "My favorite place, noon!" – it was in Lydia's handwriting. She was safe!

"This is an old note, I already saw it. I left it on the door so whoever left it would know I wasn't going to meet them," I lied, hoping Jim would believe me. I had never seen the note before, but it re-assured me that Lydia had indeed made it. She was a dear friend, and my life would be very dull without her.

"Late as it is, I think a motel would be best. Tomorrow I will contact a friend and see if I can stay with her. You don't need to follow me, I'll be fine."

As he passed me, I caught a whiff of his aftershave – Old Spice! Same scent my father used. There was something comforting and familiar about it. I shook myself and hurried to throw some things in my suitcase. My cosmetics and toiletries were still packed from my recent stay at one of the casinos on the Mississippi Gulf Coast. It took less than five minutes before I was out of the door and in my car headed, I did not know where.

Oh yes, someone was following me. I took a turn onto Brickyard Road, cutting my headlights and slipped into the dead end at Jefferson Road. Brickyard Road went across the tracks and merged with North 11th Street Extension and from there into town. My follower went the logical way across the tracks and into Ponchatoula. I carefully backed out of the driveway I had used and returned the way I had come. I took a series of backroads to the interstate and headed for Covington, about 23 miles east.

I spent a tortured night at a motel in Covington, imagining all sorts of awful things. I called my friend Libbie and asked her to pick up Nipper for a few days. So, I felt secure on that front. Lydia had left a note to tell me how to meet her. Where was her favorite place? She loved the casino, and there were security guards all around. No, that was too open.

She sang karaoke at several local bars. The next morning, I headed west toward Killian to a small bar she liked. It was down an isolated winding road lined with camps and ended at a boat launch.

Even knowing where it was, I had a hard time finding it. It was bigger than I had imagined. A nice-looking girl was alone behind the bar drying cleaned glasses.

"Are you Lynn?"

She raised an eyebrow at me as she looked me over.

"I'm Lydia's friend," I blurted out hurriedly. "I'm looking for her. Did she come here recently? I need to find her and help her if she's in trouble."

"Who's your friend?"

I turned quickly, but I smelled the Old Spice before I saw Jim smiling smugly at me.

"How did you find me?" I asked, glaring at him.

His smile broadened, and he shrugged his shoulders. He made me so mad! I needed to sit down and calm myself. I was shaking.

Lynn kept on drying glasses, listening to my tirade, and seeing that I was terribly upset.

"How about a cup of coffee on the house?" she offered.

She must have felt sorry for me or maybe my dejection showed on my face. It was a nice gesture, and I knew Lydia liked her, so I agreed.

"I'd like one, too!" Jim said and sat down at the bar with me.

Lynn served him first and then me. I saw some writing on the napkin she put under my coffee mug and discretely scrunched it up in my fist. I could recognize that writing anywhere. Lydia had left me another note. Jim was fixing his coffee and did not see the exchange.

"Where's the ladies' room?" I asked.

Lynn pointed to the back. Jim got up to follow me, and I gave him a withering look which made him sit down to resume drinking his coffee.

The ladies' room was plain but had a nice window for me to escape. It smelled of fresh Lysol. I uncrumpled my napkin and read:

"Bob and I are trying our luck at marriage. Hope we win big time."

Oh no! She would not be that stupid. I had been, but I was very young when I fell for Bob's charms. Then it dawned on me – she had not! She was telling me where they went.

It was always a big joke with her. The Las Vegas Casino and Resort was a hole in-the-wall truck stop and motel. Lydia always said the only luck a girl

154

had there was a chance of a quickie "marriage" with an instant divorce at checkout time. I never knew of her trying it, but it always made us smile.

How to get to her would be a challenge. Jim had obviously put a tracking device on my car. He had no other way of knowing where I was. I was very careful to see that no one was following me to this bar.

I pulled back the curtain to see if I could leave through the window. Nope, too far off the ground for an older person like myself. Then I saw it. Lydia's car was parked out back. She must have left the note and went off in Bob's car. She had a silver Chevy compact that looked like every other silver car on the road except for the hot pink fuzzy dice very visible through the windshield. She said it helped her find her car at Wal-Mart and other large parking lots. I had her spare key in my purse, just as she had my spare car key.

Now the problem was how to lose Jim. As if on cue, a knock on the door and Jim's voice brought me back to my current predicament.

"Are you okay?"

Guess I took too long. He needed assurance I was still there.

"Fine," I answered, as I flushed the napkin note and headed out. Losing Jim might be harder than I thought. Lynn was all alone at the bar, so no help from her.

When I came out, I sat down to finish my coffee. Lynn looked at me hard. Then she asked Jim if he would change the light in the storeroom. She gave him the bulb and step ladder when he reluctantly agreed.

"You have five minutes," she told me as she shut and bolted the storeroom door. Jim shouted and punched on the locked door, as I fled for the rear parking lot and Lydia's car. As I groped in the side compartment of my purse for the key, I found an unusual item I had not put there. Must be Jim's tracking device! I tossed it in the bed of a moving pickup and slid into Lydia's car.

I drove to the front lot and quickly retrieved my overnight bag and makeup. Speeding through the backroads, I came out on Highway 22 and headed to the nearest exit that would take me to the interstate going toward Baton Rouge and further west.

I smiled thinking of Jim chasing the pickup to some remote fishing camp. Thank you, Lynn! Lydia was right to trust her. Once over the Mississippi

River bridge, I stopped at a McDonald's for breakfast. I called my friend Libbie to be sure she had picked up Nipper at my house.

"Nipper is having a big time playing with the cats. She was out in the dog yard when I pulled up. I did not have to call her. I pulled over down the street to answer my cell phone and saw the cable truck pull into your yard. I guess you will have your cable fixed when you get back. Do not worry about your dog Nipper. I'll spoil her rotten."

"Thanks, Libbie. Don't feed her too well, or she'll turn her nose up at dog food for a week when I get back."

Oh no! I did not have TV service. I was smart to evacuate last night. I would not want to have to deal with the phony cable men. My car was at the bar, my house was probably now as messed up as Lydia's. I was on my way to a no-tell motel chasing my least favorite male and my best friend. Life could not get much worse than this.

As I left the McDonald's, the heat of the Louisiana summer hit me hard. I was in hell it seemed, and all because of Bob. How much my life had changed in such a short time. As I drove west down Highway 190, my mood got even darker.

The ditches were filled with brackish water and green spear-like leaves of iris and sedges. Large stretches of desolate highway were dotted with bleak looking houses and an occasional store. The interstate had taken most of the traffic, leaving the area with a look of desperation and poverty. Maybe it was my mood that colored the area a shade of dismal that it did not normally wear. Think of something nice, I told myself.

I smiled remembering how I outmaneuvered Jim. A memory of his Old Spice made me wish he were still with me. Oh well, he attracted me, but we had no future together. I tried to put him out of my mind. The miles passed, and I found myself still daydreaming about him. Maybe I needed to get a real life and quit thinking about strange, good looking men.

The casino signs started marking off the miles. Soon, it loomed out of the wasteland, all neon and glitzy. Part of it was a truck stop and diner, then the larger addition had the games and motel. I hoped Lydia and Bob were there and that I had guessed correctly from Lydia's note.

It was not quite noon, and the vast lobby seemed even larger with no people milling around. A portly older man nodded sleepily at the desk. A large red lipstick lip print showed as his bald head lowered closer to the desktop while he snored. It looked like Lydia's shade of pink to me.

"Hello!" I said loudly enough to wake the desk clerk. "I'm looking for Lydia Dalton."

"No one here by that name," he said, peering closely at his computer screen. "But I couldn't tell you her room number if she were here. Confidentiality, you know."

"That looks like her lipstick on the top of your head."

"Oh!" he said, touching the top of his head and smiling at a cherished memory of the event. "This must be for you."

Not another note – I must have missed Lydia and Bob thanks to Jim's shenanigans. Then I heard it – a hearty laugh that rippled over your heart and made you smile inside. No one enjoyed life more than Lydia.

I glanced at the note and saw a room number on it. Quickly, I went into the gaming area and found Lydia and my bad boy Bob. He looked tired but happy. Lydia was sipping a bloody Mary and feeling no pain.

"Lydia won big bucks! I asked her to marry me!"

"Maybe you should wait until she's sober to ask her!"

"What kept you?" Lydia said grinning at me. I was so happy to see her that I forgot all my previous bitterness. I gave her a bone crushing hug and a big kiss.

"What about me," Bob asked. "Don't I get a hug too?"

"Not on your life! Do you realize what trouble you caused Lydia and me? Her house was trashed beyond recognition, and mine is probably in the same condition. I ought to turn you in to No Neck Nick or at least to Jim Bradford."

"Who's Jim Bradford,"

"He's the private investigator hired to find you and get back what you took from Nick."

"I wonder who hired him. Nick has his own men to track and recover."

I smelled the Old Spice! Jim had tracked me down again! I turned and tried to be cool, calm, and collected, but I think my voice trembled a bit.

"Hi, Jim, you must have put two tracking devices in my purse"

"At least!" he grinned. Despite my earlier fantasizing, I felt like punching him hard, extremely hard. He was so irritating.

"Do I get a hug and a big kiss too?" he asked, crushing me in his tight grip and kissing me on the mouth.

I was too tired and too surprised to try to push him back. The Old Spice was even more fragrant so close-up. I kissed him back. Lydia was grinning, but Bob was looking sulky. Lydia found a nearby couch and curled up for a nap leaving Bob and me to sort out the problem.

"Bob, what is on the flash drive that is so important? Is it payoff information? A duplicate set of books?"

"No, it's a sex tape. A video with Nick as not many have seen him. If his wife gets hold of it, Nick could lose his cash cow. She is the one with the money that he uses to run his operation. He signed a pre-nuptial agreement that he would be faithful, and that if she wanted out, she would have to divide their assets with him. Of course, if she can prove he is sleeping around, she gets his whole operation since she's the main backer."

"Jim, are you working for Nick's wife?"

Jim turned his head away and said nothing.

"Oh, right! Your client confidentiality thing."

"Bob, why don't you give Nick's wife the tape? She might even give you a finder's fee."

"If I do that, then Nick will make mincemeat out of me."

"Then you have to find someone he's sleeping with that will blow the whistle on him. Who is in the tape?"

"Um, I don't know his name..."

"You can't be serious!"

Lydia sat up just then, "I think I can help you out."

"Lydia, tell me you didn't sleep with Nick!"

Bob looked horrified. I was aghast. Jim was interested.

"Heck no! Bob's the only loser I slept with that you know. I am talking my old friend Dominick. He's a silent partner in this casino. He has connections. He could help us."

"I need to know what you are going to do about our situation," I asked Bob. "My life's a mess and all because of you, rotten bastard that you are! You are not really going to marry Lydia and mess her life up more than you have. Where is Lydia, anyway?"

The couch was empty. We moved in a group to the front desk where Lydia and the old guy were laughing together.

"I checked out," Lydia said smiling.

"Where's the money?" Bob asked eagerly.

Lydia produced a handful of hundreds.

"Is that all?" Bob asked, alarm in his voice.

"Yes, Glenn only had $800 in the drawer, so I took $500. I did not want to break him. Where else can I feel at home and gamble all weekend. When I lose, he spots me money."

Glenn must be the old geezer half asleep at the front desk. Lydia knew everyone. Bob was reeling. Lydia was not looking like the bride he envisioned. In fact, her appeal bottomed out for him when he realized that she did not really win a lot of cash. It was just like playing monopoly, you exerted lots of time with no real reward.

My mind glazed over. I was away from my home that I enjoyed so much, chased by a sleezy bookie, and I almost missed what Lydia was saying.

By now, it was getting late. I was hungry and tired. Lydia suggested we go to the truck stop diner and have supper before getting rooms at the casino. The diner had steam trays of food that looked left over from Monday's lunch, and today was Thursday. I ate a salad which was not too wilted. Everyone else got hamburgers.

Back at the motel part of the complex, Glenn was signing me into a double occupancy room. Despite my protests to the contrary, Jim insisted he needed to keep an eye on me. I was too emotionally and physically drained to contest it. Maybe the Old Spice clouded my decision.

Jim stayed to his side of the room, though I was not sure whether to be disappointed or not. Breakfast was a sober event as each of us mulled over our individual situations. Dominick was supposed to meet us at 10 a.m., and it was already 9:30.

When we finished and went back to the hotel, I saw the back of a stubby, short statured man talking to Glenn. Lydia let out a squeal and rushed to hug him. She kissed him so hard, I felt embarrassed for her.

My ex-husband Bob was looking very pale and started backing out of the door. Jim was looking very puzzled. What had I missed?

Lydia introduced the man as Dominick or Nickie for short. She and Glenn were smiling at him, so I smiled too and offered my hand.

"You, greaseball," he said to Bob, "what do you think you're doing with my flash drive?"

"This is your bookie?" Lydia and I both said at the same time.

"Lydia, remember that time we were playing dress up sex? You dressed like a guy? I taped the role playing for kicks so I could watch it again. You know how much I enjoy our times together?" Nick said. "Well, this bozo got a hold of the flash drive, and will probably try to blackmail me with it."

"Bob! You would not do that to Nickie and me? Would you?"

"Honestly, I didn't watch it all the way through and didn't realize it was you, Lydia, honey."

"Give it back to Nickie if he promises me to destroy it!"

"Okay, Lydia, I put it over the doorsill when I went to Ponchatoula."

"Not there," Jim the detective offered. "I looked there for the key."

"You said the flowerpot was the first place you looked!"

Jim just shrugged and smiled.

"Who are these two, Lydia?" Nick demanded.

"She's my friend I told you about, and he's a detective your wife hired."

"If my flash drive isn't over the door where Bob put it, where is it?"

Why was everyone looking at me? I could not let Lydia be the third party to a messy divorce scandal. Bob was a bastard, but he did not need to have his legs broken by Nick. Why was this happening to me?

"Jim, here's a five-dollar bill, I would like to retain your services and your confidentiality. I flushed the flash drive down the toilet and now I have nothing to return to Nick. Could you possibly tell Nick's wife, that there is no flash drive? It would be the truth." I said, crossing my fingers behind my back, planning to destroy the flash drive at the first opportunity.

"You plan to buy my silence for $5? Hey, I'm a man of principle." Jim said, smiling. "Maybe if you sweeten the pot by going out with me, I might consider doing just that."

"Not so fast," Nick countered. "How do I know the flash drive was destroyed?"

"I would never jeopardize Lydia at any cost. You have to trust me on this."

"I don't live by trust in my occupation. However, from what Lydia said about your friendship, I might make a concession. Now, Bob, promise me you will break up with my sister Patty? I do not like you and do not want you as a brother-in-law. Do I make myself clear?"

It was a relieved Bob who agreed unconditionally to end his time with Patty. He had tired of the relationship like all the others he had been in, like he had tired of our marriage.

"Jim," Nick said, "I could use a discreet private detective like you. How about working for me?"

Jim smiled, imagining all the cases he could get through Nick.

"Okay, doll," Jim said to me as he tucked my five dollars into his pocket, "how about we go back to our room!"

I guess we had just started the dating part of our deal. That is until Jim's phone rang, and I heard a lot of "yes, dear's" which prompted me to ask – "The old ball and chain?" Jim blushed, having been caught. Yippee, I was off the hook without having to renege on my promise.

* * * * *

A year passed since the time Lydia and Bob led us on that wild trip. Lydia resumed her work with FEMA and was now working in Puerto Rico. Despite the long, tiring hours struggling with the language barrier, she made time to party and meet new friends.

Sweet talking, lying, cheating Bob married an older woman whose wealth made her very charming and endearing to him. I'm sure he still slipped out when he could. Nick made some serious money in his role as a bookie and his wife forgave him the past. I dropped all communication with Jim, so who knows what happened to him.

I was at the Corner Café one morning for breakfast, and the owner Kathy came over with a note. Not again! I almost didn't take it from her, but curiosity pushed me to accept it.

"Thank you so much for tutoring our daughter, Angela. She passed her math test with flying colors. Breakfast today is our treat."

I looked across the room and there sat the beaming family smiling at me. See, all notes are not bad after all.

Vicky Fannaly

Prose

By Clyde Eschete

The Christmas Tree

Jim and Doris were settled in for their first December way out in the wilderness of Alaska.

The two-room cabin with a kitchen was cozy and warm but it was lacking something.

"You know," Jim said, "it's that time of year for Santa and all that good stuff and we need a Christmas tree, especially since this is our first Christmas in our cabin. I think I'll go out and look for one."

Doris reluctantly handed his coat to Jim saying, "I wish you'd change your mind. The weather report said we're in for severe weather. It looks like a blizzard will be here before nightfall."

"Oh, don't worry," Jim replied, "With all this forest, I won't have to go far and I'll be back in about an hour."

But once on his snowmobile in the midst of so many trees, it was hard to make a decision and Jim was getting farther from home all the time.

Finally he spotted just the right tree, stopped his snowmobile, and got off, carrying his chainsaw but leaving his rifle behind.

This tree is the one! he decided.

It was only five feet tall and just right for the cabin.

The chainsaw started without any problem and Jim was able to cut the tree down easily and tie it to the back of the snowmobile.

By now, the weather was looking very threatening and snow was coming down hard.

Everything was going well until he started back to retrieve his chainsaw.

163

Suddenly something beneath him gave a loud "snap" and fastened itself around his foot, bringing with it pain greater than he had ever experienced in his whole life.

He had stepped into a bear trap hidden under the snow and the "snap" was not only the sounds of the jaws of the trap he had triggered, but the severing of bone.

The pain was so great, he passed out.

When he finally came to, he lay there for a good while.

I'm in a whole lot of trouble, he thought.

He was already cold but the next sound he heard was enough to freeze him with fear – it was wolves off in the distance.

Jim knew a wolf could smell blood at least five miles away when they were downwind.

And, he knew he didn't have any choice in what he had to do.

He said aloud in agony, "God, this is going to hurt, but not as much as when those wolves get here before I can get to my rifle."

Removing his gloves with trembling hands, he managed to reach the other boot and untie the boot string, using it as a tourniquet.

Taking out his knife, he made two cuts above the ankle and, using sawing strokes, cut off his foot between the broken bones.

Overwhelmed with uncontrollable pain, after ten minutes or so, Jim began crawling and dragging himself inches at a time, trying to get to the safety of his snowmobile and rifle before the fast-approaching wolves arrived.

He had just pulled up on the seat of the snowmobile when the first wolf appeared out of the trees.

Jim grabbed the rifle, trying to focus and aim at the same time.

So weak he didn't know if he could do either one, he was surprised when he pulled the trigger, heard a yelp and watched the wolf fall.

He had killed it!

Thankfully, the snowmobile started and Jim sped down an almost-invisible trail with four other wolves in hot pursuit.

After a mile or so, they just gave up and dropped back to investigate their dead leader.

When Jim spotted the cabin through the falling snow, he felt relief, knowing he would be okay.

And almost at the door, he turned off the motor and collapsed, unconscious.

When he woke up, he was in the hospital, and found Doris seated at his side.

He looked over at her with a frown and said, "Enjoy this Christmas tree because it is the last one we will ever have if *I'*m the one to go out and cut it down."

The End

The Gnome

It was Saturday morning and Lilly was up at six o 'clock.

After fixing coffee and toast for breakfast, she went out to the porch to retrieve her morning paper.

Opening it filled her with excitement as she went straight to the section listing garage sales.

Pouring over every listing, she finally said out loud, "This is the one!"

Lilly always tried to be the first to arrive for the best buys, or so she thought.

Quickly gathering her purse and keys, she jumped into the front seat of her jeep and in half an hour, she had reached her destination.

As usual, she was first.

Much to her surprise, it was a big sale. Even bigger than it had appeared in the paper.

After smiling and greeting some of the families who'd gone together to have the sale, she thought to herself, *Look at all the nice things I have to choose from this morning for my garden!*

Right away she started work at filling her basket.

On the ground at the end of the first aisle, she noticed a funny-looking gnome.

He was small with a pointed head and a weird, odd-shaped beard. He was splattered with mud but she picked him up anyhow for a closer look.

Just one dollar.

Not being that interested, she put the gnome back.

But, turning the corner to the next aisle, right at the first was another funny-looking gnome on the ground.

Oh, good! There are two of them, she exclaimed silently. I'm going to get them both and put one on each end of my garden.

So, she picked it up and put it in her basket.

She went back to the first aisle to get the matching gnome.

It wasn't there!

I'm sure it was on this aisle, she told herself. And the other shoppers walking up haven't been over here yet.

166

Lilly walked around looking for the other gnome but had no luck.

When checking out, she said, "I'd like to buy the other gnome that looks just like this one. I've looked everywhere but, I can't find it again."

"I'm sorry, M'am, but that's the only one we have."

Lilly was surprised by his answer and said, frowning, "Are you sure?"

"Yes, M'am."

Smiling anyhow, Lilly loaded all the treasures she had bought into her jeep.

Just as I thought, early birds do get the best of everything.

When she arrived home, she was almost jumping with joy and hurried to her shed for the wheelbarrow to hold everything she'd bought.

I have all day tomorrow to arrange all my new things in the garden. It's time for lunch anyway.

Singing with happiness she walked to the house pushing her loaded wheelbarrow to set inside the garage.

In the kitchen, Lilly went to the sink to wash her hands.

When she turned around, she was surprised to find the gnome sitting at the end of the table.

She gasped and cried out, "How did that filthy thing get in here on my table?"

Picking it up, she walked over to the back door and threw it outside onto the grass.

After washing her hands a second time, she turned around and, much to her disbelief, the gnome was sitting on the end of the table again.

This time, the hairs on the back of her neck rose.

She shouted aloud, "What in the hell is going on? Did I imagine this?"

Being so disturbed and confused, Lilly could barely make it to a chair to sit down. It seemed to her the gnome's eyes followed her as she'd walked from the sink to the chair.

His beard moved as if he were smiling.

He peered at Lilly and declared, "You, my dear, bought me. Now you own me for life. Wherever you go or whatever you do, I will always be with you."

I must be hallucinating! That damn thing can't be talking to me! I'm going to pick him up and throw him out again.

Closing the kitchen's outside door, she started to fix her lunch.

But as she turned around to put her sandwich on the table, she found the gnome standing on the end of the table again.

All the blood drained from her face.

I am going to finish this once and for all!

After grabbing him with shaking hands, Lilly went out to the garden and grabbed a shovel. She dug a hole and threw him in it.

After covering him with dirt, she shouted, "That should be the end of you!"

Hurrying back inside, Lilly was alarmed and frightened to see him back on the end of the table!

She was so traumatized, she just walked out of the kitchen and left the gnome there.

In the living room, she sat and lit a cigarette.

Leaning back in the chair, she closed her eyes and thought, Oh, no! I haven't smoked in three weeks! I am not going to start back now!

When she opened her eyes to put the cigarette out, whom did she see?

That gnome was now on the coffee table looking at her.

All she could do was sit there staring at him.

What am I going to do! I can't call anyone. They'll think I'm crazy!

Everywhere she went in the house, he was there. All afternoon and into the night, the gnome followed Lilly.

Lilly screamed out loud, "I just can't take this anymore!"

Bolting into her bedroom, she threw herself onto the bed and soon fell into a deep and exhausted sleep.

Sunday morning, Lilly jolted up in bed before daybreak, her blouse wringing wet.

Sweat was dripping off the end of her nose.

She whispered, "Thank goodness it was only a nightmare."

Out of the darkness, she heard that voice from her nightmare and started shaking like a leaf in the wind.

Grasping her head with her hands, thinking it was about to explode, she cried out, "It's *not* a nightmare!"

The same raspy voice whispered, "Don't be afraid, my dear. Mr. McGlone is right here. I will be with you for as long as you live."

Lilly jumped out of bed, running across the room to turn on the light.
There he was, as big as day, in the corner!

Lilly was so upset, she walked the floor all that day and most of the night.
Completely worn out, she went to her bedroom and collapsed on the bed.
By six in the morning, she had drifted off to sleep.

When she finally woke up, seeing the late morning sunlight already streaming in the window, she jumped up.

Oh, no!! I'm late again!!

Frowning, Lilly looked over at the gnome. In a voice dripping with sarcasm, she declared, "You're supposed to take care of me. Well, then, why didn't you wake me up."

Knowing she was in trouble at work and still half asleep, Lilly hurriedly threw water in her face. In the kitchen, she took a few minutes to drink a cup of coffee.

Running outside, she jumped in the jeep to head to work.

She was still in a stupor but petrified, seeing the gnome was right there next to her on the front seat.

While driving to work, she prayed the gnome would not appear in the office with her.

After parking her car, Lilly decided the best solution was to put the gnome in her tote bag so he wouldn't appear in the office where her co-workers would see him.

She arrived at work two hours late.

Stapled to her time card was a note from the owner, not a good omen, especially when she read in bold letters, **"See me before you clock in today."**

Her stomach was in a knot as she walked into his office.

The owner looked up at Lilly and flatly stated, "I warned you that the next time you arrived late for work you would lose your job. Here's your pay. That is all."

After leaving his office, she sat in her car and cried. She uttered in between sobs, "What am I to do!"

The gnome had appeared on the seat next to her again.

He said in a compassionate voice, "Lilly, my dear, stop crying. As you must take care of me, I am obliged to take care of you. Go to the nearest store and buy a power-ball ticket. Only play the numbers I give you. Your troubles will soon be over."

After all that's happened, I feel like I'm crazy. So, I'm going to buy that damn power-ball ticket out of curiosity. The ticket costs only two dollars.

Stopping at the first store she came to on her way home, Lilly bought the ticket.

Arriving home, she went into the kitchen to wash her hands before fixing herself a cup of coffee.

As usual, there the gnome was on the end of the table.

Lilly reached over, picked him up, and put him in the sink.

While washing all the mud off Mr. McGlone, she looked down at him and said with resignation, "The least I can do is clean you up."

It was Tuesday night.

Lilly sat on the sofa with Mr. McGlone seated next to her, waiting for the news to announce the power-ball numbers.

There on the TV screen were all the numbers he'd told her to play.

Just as he'd predicted, they *were* the winning numbers.

Lilly jumped up off the sofa and picking up Mr. McGlone, she danced

Mr. McGlone looked up at Lilly with a twinkle in his eye and said, "I told you your troubles would be over."

"You are magical, Mr. McGlone!"

Still, with a measure of disbelief, Lilly inquired, "How old are you?"

"My dear Lilly, I existed long before there were any kings."

After Tuesday night, Lilly and Mr. McGlone made plans to travel the

On their first flight to Europe the stewardess noticed the gnome wearing a seat belt on the seat next to Lilly. She frowned and asked Lilly, "What is that doing on the seat next to you?"

Smiling, Lilly looked up and answered, "Don't worry about him. I paid for his seat."

Lilly and Mr. McGlone traveled the world for the next fifty years.

As he'd promised, the gnome never left her side.

The End

Prose and Poetry

By Tracey Boyle

Darling Buds of May

"I'll set the tea up on the patio. Such a pleasant day." Gemma smiles at her father-in-law. "Mia is anxious for her walk about the garden."

John looks down at his three-year-old granddaughter. "Mrs. Randolph brought a cake, there, on the sideboard."

"Of course. You go on now."

John takes Mia's small and delicate hand into his, feeling privileged for the visit. Gemma had begun to come for weekly visits on Sundays, while Peter was playing golf. A few months ago, John had finally met his little granddaughter. 'I would like to know my father-in-law,' Gemma had said, when he opened the door that first time. This was after Gemma had seen him entering the cancer center, although it took three visits before she brought it up.

They walk across the bright green lawn. Mia skips along at John's side, stopping to touch the silken petals of tulips growing in the herbaceous border. The birds celebrate the gorgeous weather, singing as if in conversation.

Hurry up. Hurry up, a Robin calls.

At the bottom of winding terrace steps, Mia pets the head of a cement pony statue. John looks up the steps and recalls a 1912 photo of Great-Grandmother sitting near newly built stone walls that were clean, sturdy, and uncluttered by various vines or flowering plants which have split and crumbled these walls over the past one hundred-plus years. Maintaining the property is a lot of work, and John worries what will become of it. He relies on garden club volunteers who exchange their hours for his hosting annual tours to raise money for their club or associated charities.

Come to me, me. Come to me, me, a Goldfinch sings.

He takes Mia's hand as they slowly ascend steps, lined on one side with flowering pots, being careful to avoid Creeping Thyme that has grown over certain spots. The view from the top terrace is one John indulges in every day, overlooking rose beds, farm buildings, and the Devonshire countryside in the distance. Next, they descend through a narrow path surrounded by a field carpeted with blooming Bluebells. Here are a few of the hundred oak trees that John's father established years ago. Buster, his chocolate Labradoodle, meets them and trots ahead, his ears flapping. Buster knows the way, and occasionally turns around to be sure he is being followed.

Be sweet. Be sweet to me, the Song Thrush beckons.

They step through an area naturalized with bulbs that have finished their annual display. When they reach the fence bordering the property, Mia places her tiny hands onto a gate's wooden railing. "Baa baaah," she mimics sheep in the distance. "Where are the little lambs?"

John holds her up in his arms. "See, there," he says pointing, and then notices Mary Randolph approaching them.

"Hello John," Mary greets him, as she props her walking stick against a fence post, then adjusts her grey curls behind her ears. "And here's a sweet one." She pats Mia's cheek. Mia sticks a finger into her mouth and turns her face into John's chest shyly. "Have you been feeling well, John?"

"Wonderful now."

"Dinner on Tuesday? Mary asks. "Bob looks forward to the Chess challenge."

"Yes, Tuesday. I'll be there. Thank you, Mary." Mary takes up her stick to continue the walk around the perimeter of her property.

I can hear you. I can hear you.

John and Mia move away from the gate resuming their walk. They scrape past a fuchsia-colored camellia bush that towers above John's six-foot frame. The gentle sound of water splashing beneath a bridge leads them to Mia's favorite spot, where a swing hangs from a huge Tulip Poplar that reigns over a garden room. John lifts Mia onto the swing and keeping his gnarled and mottled hands over her plump, soft ones, John gives her a gentle push, looking into the eyes of May.

. . . May . . . his May . . .

Gone from his bed one freezing, snowy, morning. Nowhere in the house, panicking, hurrying to search the large property, visioning May frozen on the ground, or face up in the stream. He hears her laughter and finds her here, where she is swinging, barefoot, in only her white gown, lips bluing. He removes his coat, wraps her up, carrying her to the house.

Racing between the kettle in the kitchen and the fireplace, poking dry sticks into a fire, rubbing May's feet, where he had propped her into a chair, covering her in blankets.

. . . her eyes recognizing . . .
"John, oh John."
. . . a moment of lucidity . . .
"Yes, I'm John, my darling May."
. . . touching her cheek . . .
"I'm so sorry – sorry for this."
"Never. Don't be."
. . . the kettle whistling . . .
. . . her look, far away . . .
"Peter, has he come by?"
. . . green eyes tearing up . . .

I feel anger, welling up from my heart to my head, and out to the ends of my fingers. Her brief moments of lucidness, wasted, on grief. Stolen - by our son!
"Don't leave me, John."
"Never. You're my May."
. . . a few happy moments . . .

Then May is gone again. I hold her two hands in my own for a time, then go to tend the kettle in the kitchen.
I'll see you soon. I'll see you soon.

John and Mia enter the apple orchard, walking through planted wildflowers, while Buster runs ahead, poking his nose into the edges of overgrown grasses, sniffing for rabbits, maybe. Some of the apple trees are covered with white flowers, promising a good harvest, while other cultivars lag behind. Like children, John thinks.

. . . like Peter . . .
. . . the row they had had . . .
. . . about him not visiting . . .
"Why? She doesn't know me."
"She has periods when she remembers."
"Not when I'm there."
"She cries. She misses you."
"Don't guilt trip me!"
"Selfish," I yell. "You owe your mother – the time!"

There were more arguments, denials, resentment; the wedge that split John and his son apart. They stood next to each other at the funeral, and never spoke a word . . . five years now.

John moves his finger beneath his eye wiping away a tear. He sees the house looming before them. He and Mia have walked full circle now. The front of the three-story, old Elizabethan manor is covered with blooms of yellow climbing roses. Buster precedes them through the open door, then through a long hallway that leads out to the patio where Gemma waits for them at a table.

Gravel crunches on the drive outside the brick wall. Maybe a garden club volunteer taking advantage of the nice weather, John thinks. He places Mia onto a chair while Gemma begins to pour the tea. The metal latch on the gate clangs. John freezes as he sees his son, Peter, dressed in a polo shirt and khaki golf pants, walking toward them. He grabs the back of a chair, his heart skips beats. John is lightheaded. All stops; no birds chirping, no tea dribbling into China cups, no perfume from Zephirine Drouhin roses climbing the brick wall, no soft, ruffling of wind to carry scent. Seeing John's reaction, and then

Peter, Gemma puts the teapot down. Looking scattered, almost fearful, she says to John, "I didn't know," as if it were her fault somehow.

He can't take his eyes off his son. The birds sing. Roses perfume the air.

"I couldn't be more pleased," he says. Then turning to look Gemma directly in the eyes, repeats, "I couldn't be more pleased." Then Peter is at the table, looking tall, healthy, with his green eyes and blond hair.

"Daddy's here!" Mia bounces in her chair.

"Father," Peter says, and warily reaches his hand out to shake John's hand.

Looking into May's eyes, John shakes Peter's hand. "Have a seat, son. You're just in time for tea." John smiles and pulls a chair out for Peter, then one for himself.

Gemma begins to pour tea again, and then cuts the cake. The clinking of silverware against China plates melds with birdsong.

"I want biscuits, Mummy, not cake," Mia insists. "Grandad, you want a biscuit too?"

John looks at his family around the table, then at the expanse of gardens and countryside surrounding the old home while the birds call out encouragingly.

Begin again. Begin again.

This story won The Olive Woolley Burt Award for first place in Short Fiction from The League of Utah Writers in 2021.

Tracey Boyle

Disappear

Where do you go
when you disappear?

When you stand at your chain-link fence
    frail shoulders bent,
    mouth working
    your gray-stubbled chin,
    gazing into your brother's yard
all these years – not speaking to him.

What do you think about?

Weeds in the garden that need to be hoed,
    trash to be put out,
    paint brushed
    stroke by stroke,
    again and again
on the walls that you built.

What do they think?

    Of an uncle they hardly know,
    about a quarrel long forgotten
    that divided family,
    of the unspeakable silence
    that grew and grew
the sadness you will take with you.

Ineffable

Words evade me.

So I search for perfect words, everywhere –

in hallways, in closets and shoe boxes,

under beds, through laundry baskets,

in the cracks between floorboards,

between pages on bookshelves, dishes piled in the sink,

in empty flower vases and dog bowls,

under doormats, and in boots left on the porch,

behind hub caps, in glove boxes, between shovels and rakes,

in smeared chalk on sidewalks, on basketball courts,

in schoolroom primers, on flyers left in grocery baskets,

between eggplants at farmers' markets,

on wooden pews, in shiny chalices,

through clouds and stained glass,

in the purring of cats and the laughter of children,

on baby's drool, and in tears of the aged.

Tracey Boyle

Fashion's Bride

-(on Dolce and Gabbana Alta Moda 2020, September Show)

Dusk
illuminating runway steps
ornamented with tuxedoed grooms,
a captivated audience hypnotized in
the soft rustle of taffeta sweeping legs,
as a promenade of dress after dress
trickles colors and petals to float
in rhythm with
ART
accenting chiseled features in
unfeeling faces veiled in netting,
bound in tulle and crowned pink roses.
Groom gently taking gloved hand,
Leading slippered feet to whisper
in harmony with violins and harp,
flowing trills of somber sighs and exclaims –
the crescendo –
glitter fading before next season's
Dawn.

Suburb Girl

Three hours to get to our cousins -
"55 Saves Lives" and no interstate
across the Atchafalaya Basin.

My aunt spoils little girls she never had -
only three brawny sons and
a powerhouse husband who drives rice combines.

Breakfast of fresh gathered eggs,
yolks more orange than store-bought,
Sunday morning church, then a
best-tasting fried chicken lunch.

A backyard of sheep and cows
in pasture as far as the eye can see.
Watch for the cow pads. Cow pads?
Horns look threatening - don't wear red.

Cat skulks out the barn door at
the foreign tinkling of girl voices.
Hay bales stacked tip-top to loft's roof,
I enter a narrow tunnel excavated by boy cousins.
Hay closing in is scary, I'm lost –

The middle cousin finds me,
moving ahead as my guide.
We exit to no space on the loft floor to walk,
except on joists.

The older brother hefts a hay bale -
used to the daily chore,

breaks it apart with a pitchfork,
dropping hay to cows below.

I look down at muddy imprints
of cows' hooves eight feet below -
I picture me falling into mucky cow slop.
"I won't let you fall."

I glance into Cajun blue eyes,
stick-straight blonde hair framing his ruddy complexion,
only two years older, but hulky -
these farm boys, strong and confident.

He takes my hand,
places his foot onto a joist with me.
"Step," he says, moving his foot to the next joist.
Waits, until I do the same.

"Step," he says.
We move forward again.
"Step," I say with him.

We continue together,
"Step."
    "Step."

"Step," I say alone.
We step again.

I'm gaining courage now.

    "Step."
        "Step."
            "Step."

Decades later –
aunt, uncle, and barn - gone,
house rented, pastures leased for
offshoremen apartments, a heliport
and crawfish farming.

Suburb girl smiles
at the Roseate Spoonbills,
scooping in to nab a meal.

Creative Minds Writers Group

What we are about:

Our goal is to establish a network of writers who serve to support, educate, and critique each other. We are also a community advocate group for literary arts and activities in the region. We accept all writers of all genres with little to no writing experience.

Come join us!